33 Strength and Fitness
WORKOUTS FOR HORSES

ALSO BY JEC ARISTOTLE BALLOU

55 Corrective Exercises for Horses

101 Dressage Exercises for Horse and Rider

101 Western Dressage Exercises for Horse and Rider

Equine Fitness

33 Strength and Fitness WORKOUTS FOR HORSES

Practical Conditioning Plans Using Groundwork, Ridden Work, Poles, Hills, and Terrain

JEC ARISTOTLE BALLOU

T
Trafalgar Square
North Pomfret, Vermont

First published in 2024 by
Trafalgar Square Books
North Pomfret, Vermont 05053

Disclaimer of Liability
The author and publisher shall have neither liability nor responsibility to any person or entity with respect to any loss or damage caused or alleged to be caused directly or indirectly by the information contained in this book. While the book is as accurate as the author can make it, there may be errors, omissions, and inaccuracies.

   Trafalgar Square Books encourages the use of approved safety helmets in all equestrian sports and activities.

Trafalgar Square Books certifies that the content in this book was generated by a human expert on the subject, and the content was edited, fact-checked, and proofread by human publishing specialists with a lifetime of equestrian knowledge. TSB does not publish books generated by artificial intelligence (AI).

Library of Congress Cataloging-in-Publication Data
Names: Ballou, Jec Aristotle, author.
Title: 33 strength and fitness workouts for horses : practical conditioning plans using
    groundwork, ridden work, poles, hills, and terrain / Jec Aristotle Ballou.
Other titles: Thirty three strength and fitness workouts for horses
Description: North Pomfret, Vermont : Trafalgar Square Books, 2024. | Includes index.
Identifiers: LCCN 2023043565 (print) | LCCN 2023043566 (ebook) | ISBN
    9781646011865 (hardcover) | ISBN 9781646012039 (epub)
Subjects: LCSH: Horses--Training. | Horses--Exercise.
Classification: LCC SF287 .B245 2024 (print) | LCC SF287 (ebook) | DDC 636.1/0835--dc23/
    eng/20240108
LC record available at https://lccn.loc.gov/2023043565
LC ebook record available at https://lccn.loc.gov/2023043566

Photos by Donna Stidolph *except:* Back-Up (throughout), Tight Serpentine (throughout), and
    4.14 D (by Tiny Dark Room)
Diagrams by Shawn Darling
Book design by Lauryl Eddlemon
Cover design by RM Didier
Index by Andrea M. Jones (www.jonesliteraryservice.com)

Printed in China

10 9 8 7 6 5 4 3 2 1

To Diamante,
the little horse with the
most generous spirit

Contents

45

56

85

97

Preface

Since my earliest years with horses, I have been intrigued by the role fitness plays in their health and performance. As a youngster, I competed in long distance trail riding aboard a spunky Welsh Cob mare who carried me to three undefeated seasons. That tough little mare planted a seed: a well-prepared body can do incredible things!

That seed later bloomed into a full-blown profession. I have made my living helping horses reach their athletic potential. As the author of multiple books related to exercising and conditioning horses, I have been blessed to hear positive feedback, over and over, from riders who have been able to improve their horses' well-being with the strategies I've shared.

Along the way, this work with horses inspired my own fitness journey. I fell in love with ultramarathon trail running, mountain bike racing, and summiting peaks. Becoming the best student I could be, I have managed to set course records, push past boundaries, and be in awe of what is possible. Again, I am reminded that a well-prepared body can do incredible things.

In the pages ahead I share some of what I know to help you give your horse the best chance at a sound, healthy, long-performing life.

Jec Aristotle Ballou
Soquel, California

PART ONE:
BEFORE YOU BEGIN

CHAPTER 1

Does Your Horse Need This Book?

Most riders possess an arsenal of useful exercises to perform with their horses. But when it comes to improving equine fitness, exercises rely not only on weekly relevance but on *dosage*—how intensely an exercise is applied, the duration and frequency of execution, and the weekly schedule within which workouts exist determines its impact on fitness. This book takes the guesswork out of fitness gains for your horse. It clarifies how long and how frequently to do given exercises, and in which combinations they are best performed. It will help you maximize your horse's athleticism.

The workouts in these pages help accomplish the performance goals that many riders strive for within their disciplines but often fall short of reaching—stronger, more agile, and more balanced horses. They do this by circumventing the tension, both physical *and* mental, that often spoils conditioning attempts made within a discipline-specific or skill-based session. By providing the right amount of stimulus while avoiding the boredom/laxity, fatigue, and habituated neuromuscular patterns that can be typical of a schooling session, these routines lead to physiological gains.

Performance Erodes without Fitness

The importance of equine fitness cannot be overstated. In terms of health, good behavior, and overall well-being, it is a critical tool in your toolbox. While it can be tempting to assume that horses make daily conditioning gains by practicing the skill sets within your chosen discipline, this fails to be the case over the long term. When performing at a similar power output, metabolic state, and duration, a horse's physiological state reaches a point of diminishing returns. Eventually, the body becomes so efficient at performing habituated routines that fitness begins to erase. Becoming more efficient means the body has practiced movement patterns so frequently that it recruits fewer muscle fibers to execute the same muscle contractions and accomplish the same gymnastic task. Without varied stimulus, previously engaged muscles become less active. Therefore, targeted bouts of stimulus that are *not* tied to skills within their discipline are what can help most horses continue gaining, or maintaining, fitness.

A useful parallel here is the human runner or hiker or cyclist whose performance begins to erode unless supportive workouts are incorporated—that is, strength work, core and posture workouts, stretching routines, and cross-training. The body needs novelty and challenges to stay attuned.

Successful workouts deliver these challenges. Their entire purpose is physical and athletic improvement. I make this simple point because many riders have a hard time letting go of their sport-specific ideals to momentarily prioritize physical conditioning. For example, your dressage horse is *not* going to be "on the bit" during a gallop set; your arena-only horse might initially become distracted during hill workouts and trail hikes; your trail horse might trip over his own feet during groundwork routines. This is all perfectly okay. Do not get lost in these details. Remember: you are not being judged; the purpose is to deliver conditioning stimulus as opposed to perfecting a performance.

1.1 "Less than perfect" is okay during conditioning workouts. Here, I don't expect Diamante's outline to resemble our dressage sessions.

Fitness Has a Protective Function

Before we get to the actual workouts, it is worth highlighting the protective role of fitness for a horse. Daily exercise controls the basic bodily functions of your horse in the following ways:

1. Aids gastrointestinal motility.
2. Increases clearance of secretions from lungs.
3. Improves immunity and resistance to disease; muscle contractions serve as a pump for lymphatic system.
4. Strengthens hooves and contributes to healthy growth.
5. Improves thermoregulation.
6. Determines functionality of muscles, tendons, and ligaments.
7. Relieves physical stiffness and mental stress associated with confinement in domesticated horses.
8. Promotes circulation for blood, oxygen, muscle enzymes, and nutrients that prevent inflammation.

To reiterate, these systems are *dependent* on sufficient exercise and activity. In other words, we owe it to our horses to keep them fit.

How to Use This Book

These workouts are meant to occur within the framework of consistent weekly training. As applies to most exercise routines, they will not be helpful in cases where a horse might be trained only one or two times per week or sporadically throughout a month.

For horses building toward baseline fitness, the Groundwork Routines for Fitness chapter (p. 40) offers suitable workouts. These routines can be used as often as wished, up to daily, to add supplemental activity to a horse's week. During periods of the year when your horse has higher fitness and you wish to lengthen the duration of a given workout, you can do this by increasing the warm-up time by 10 to 20 minutes or adding extra time walking and jogging to cool down.

Horses with an established baseline fitness will benefit primarily from Chapters 5 and 6 (pp. 72 and 88), although groundwork exercises in Chapter 4 (p. 40) can be included throughout the week to add variety, improve relaxation and flexibility, or add activity to days off. Allow your specific goals and horse's aptitude to guide your choices.

Unless consulting with a physiotherapist, trusted trainer, or vet, you will want to observe the following general parameters:

1. Perform routines from Chapter 3 up to several days weekly.
2. Perform workouts from Chapters 4 or 5 *once* weekly.

The purpose of these workouts is to deliver the type of condensed stimulus that leads to physiological adaptations. The purpose is *not* to repeat a favorite session over and over. A good rule of thumb is to swap your workout routine every two weeks. This allows the horse enough practice and familiarity to perform it well, without tension or anxiety, before moving on to a different stimulus. For example, I might choose to do *Workout 17: The 4x3* (p. 81), with my horse on two consecutive weeks. Then, the following week, I would choose a different workout.

Strength-based workouts are intentionally short compared to endurance-type workouts. Their structure includes about 10 to 20 minutes of hard cumulative work supported by a warm-up, cooldown, and strategic rest periods. During the initial reps of an exercise, the nervous system recruits a calibrated number of muscle fibers. As some of those fibers fatigue, others are recruited to complete the task. At lower intensities of exercise, a higher number of reps are required to engage the greatest percentage of fibers. At higher intensities of exercise, fewer reps are needed to recruit the most fibers.

Determining a Horse's Level of Fitness

When we talk about strength, we refer to a horse's overall durability and his capability to perform with ease and efficiency. This includes everything from strong hooves and muscular tone to good posture and movement, plus a lot in between.

Choosing what to do with a horse any given day depends on knowing his current fitness level. In order to make gains from targeted workouts, he already needs the neuromuscular adaptations acquired from a *baseline fitness*. This ensures that the neuromuscular

1.2 Groundwork helps maintain fitness during poor weather and less riding.

system receives, and recovers from, the intended stimulus, as opposed to flooding the system with acidity (*metabolic waste byproduct*) and inconsistent fiber recruitment.

What is *baseline fitness*? To maintain the physiological state and metabolic pathways to exercise without hardship, horses need to exercise a minimum of three to four days per week on a consistent basis. *This figure includes horses that live in pasture.* Horses at this level of activity for six weeks, assuming their sessions last 25 or more minutes and include a variety of intensity, can be said to have a *baseline fitness*. From here, targeted workouts like the ones in Chapters 4 and 5 help the horse make significant and continued gains, rather than hitting a plateau.

When training regularity decreases, horses begin to lose measurable fitness markers after four weeks of less exercise than usual. Horses do not maintain fitness with fewer than three sessions per week. Their generous spirit and lack of complaint must not be mistaken for adapted physiology.

As a general rule, when a layoff has lasted more than two months, the same amount of time the horse has been *out* of work will be required to *reintroduce* work. For example, if a horse has been off for 12 weeks, allow 12 weeks of reconditioning to achieve prior fitness. This is especially important for reducing stress on the lower limbs. When the skeletal muscles have lost tone and activity, there is greater stress on the lower limbs, which often results in ligament injuries.

What If Your Horse Lives at Pasture?

A pastured horse has advantages when it comes to the speed with which he makes conditioning gains compared to a mostly stabled horse. Above all, the flexibility and tone of his back will be in far better shape. This is due to being able to wander around with a lowered neck position all day, which positively tractions the ligament system that stabilizes and engages his back in a healthy posture. This also facilitates greater mobility between vertebrae and helps eliminate the crowding of vertebrae that leads to stiffness and discomfort. Other areas of his body are also apt to be more mobile, like his ribcage and neck. Likely, the added movement in his daily life will also lead to heightened proprioception and a more "awake" nervous system that will make quicker adaptations to conditioning.

While indeed critical for overall wellness, pasture living does not, however, directly translate to fitness. It is best seen as a *supplement* to daily exercise versus a replacement to it. Horses move around their pastures with random bursts of internally motivated energy. These spurts differ from sustained movement in three basic ways:

1. Neuromuscular coordination.
2. Muscle contractions.
3. Cell metabolism.

Neuromuscular Coordination

Carrying out an activity for any length of time beyond a couple of minutes requires a well-grooved pattern of nerve signals triggering the same muscles with consistent impulse. The sensory nerves communicate the position of joints and limbs to the central nervous system, and the motor nerves, meanwhile, send stimulus to the muscles needed to keep moving them. These pathways of communication do not automatically exist. They develop over a period of training and conditioning, one that lasts at least six weeks. Until then, a horse's best effort under saddle will be inconsistent moments of decent movement. These moments will likely be sporadic and unsustainable.

Muscle Contractions

For a horse to maintain his own balance with a rider on top, he must engage a certain amount of muscle contraction in the muscles of the neck and hindquarters. These contractions are needed to stabilize his spine and pelvis while moving and carrying a rider. An *isometric contraction* is defined as a muscle tensioning while holding its normal length. By nature, a horse's muscular system is not designed very well for these kinds of contractions. As a prey animal, his muscles evolved to favor short bursts of energy to run from a predator and then stop moving.

Keeping a muscle under sustained pressure, as is the case of the neck muscles when trying to stabilize an unfit horse's back carrying a rider, builds up burning irritation of nerve endings. The metabolic waste generated as the muscles try to work through this "pools up," stagnates, and causes soreness. Over time, a horse's muscles *can* be improved to hold isometric contractions, but this does not happen without conditioning.

Cell Metabolism

Over the course of intentional conditioning, muscles become more adapted to utilize calcium and magnesium, along with other elements, to generate contraction-relaxation cycles efficiently. They also improve their ability to flush out lactate and waste byproducts that are the result of energy production. Meanwhile, as plasma volumes increase in the conditioned horse, there is a greater delivery of blood and oxygen to muscles to support these functions. Simultaneously, capillary beds become denser, which improves blood supply to muscles. Furthermore, sustained exercises delivered by a conditioning program increase the *mitochondria* in cells, the little structures referred to as "power plants" that produce energy for muscles to contract. As mitochondria density improves, muscles can work more efficiently for longer periods of time.

Different Fitness Types

The term "fitness" is often applied broadly within horse training, but it deserves a specific use. Like humans, horses can possess different types of fitness. To go further with the human analogy, a power weightlifter has an entirely different type of fitness than a distance runner. A ballerina and a power-lifting athlete are both fit, but their fitness differs in terms of the physiological systems it enhances. Using the term "fit" to describe an equine body that is accustomed to exercise is vague and unhelpful when choosing workouts. Are the bones and hooves well adapted? Do the muscles possess power or stamina? Or some measure of both? Is the metabolic system capable of reaching maximum aerobic threshold?

When discussing a particular horse's fitness, we should be clear what type of fitness is being referred to. Most simply, you can think of three areas: *cardiovascular, strength,* and *coordination/proprioception*. The latter area is relevant mostly for youngsters or horses rehabbing from injury but also applies to very unfit horses during early phases of training.

Horses are remarkable athletes. Their physiology makes them highly adaptable to cardiovascular gains. Within several weeks of beginning exercise, most horses show measurable improvement in plasma volume, capillary beds, heart and respiratory rates, and mitochondria. This all results in better blood flowing to muscles, fatigue resistance, energy, and recovery from exercise.

Compared to humans, horses adapt much more readily to cardiovascular training. In the area of strength (which is related to the musculoskeletal system), however, horses take much longer to adapt compared to their metabolic gains. To use an automobile analogy, many horses have powerful engines (cardiovascular system) on a weak or failing chassis (musculoskeletal system). It is in the areas of strength (musculoskeletal fitness) and coordination/proprioception (neuromotor fitness) that many horses need to improve the most.

The workouts in this book target these areas. It would be inaccurate to claim they are entirely non-cardio, but bear in mind that the goal of these routines is not to reach peak cardio fitness. The horse *might* get quite winded during the 1:1 Intervals (p. 79), for instance, but our purpose is not to improve his heart and lungs to race around a track. Instead, these intervals are intended to increase muscle power and stamina.

1.3 I add movement to Corazon's day with valuable proprioceptive exercises in the afternoon after our morning ride.

These are the types of gains that help him travel with more ease and comfort, perform collected movements, or tackle the next hill on your trail ride efficiently.

Value and Vigor

Productive exercise can take all kinds of forms, and it is worth remembering that it is not just the work you do when practicing your discipline or having a lesson that counts. The body benefits from differing intensities, both short *and* long sessions, novel patterns of joint flexion, precise motor control as well as big propulsive efforts. In sum, there is a broad scope of beneficial ways to move your horse daily beyond the trappings of your normal routine.

A productive session is not necessarily measured by its vigor. Good workouts should be *valuable* to the horse, not just tire him out or create a lot of sweat. Workouts should begin by asking oneself, "What does this horse *need*?" Does he need a dose of strong hard effort like gallop intervals or hill climbs to fire up the hindquarter muscles? Does he need long interval sets to increase stamina in his working gaits? Or does he need a routine to activate the body but release tension and stiffness?

Sometimes a brisk 2-mile walk down the road followed by several purposeful groundwork exercises is just what the body needs to loosen up and engage core muscles. Other times, a session of gymnastic jumps can deliver powerful stimulus to muscles that have become overused and stiff from dressage. My point in offering these examples is to encourage you to think broadly about the variety of both small and large workouts that help a body thrive.

By asking yourself what the horse needs on a weekly and daily basis, you will avoid the pitfalls of repetitive movement, which not only undermines physical conditioning but predisposes the horse to injury and restricted gaits. Most horses, even those in a regular training program, benefit from additional periods of movement in their day. This keeps the body's soft tissues pliable, the muscles oxygenated, and the nerve signals primed.

2

Structuring Your Week

Regardless of whether the goal is to maintain a horse's fitness or increase it, you cannot do the same thing every day. Otherwise, as I explained in chapter 1, the body *loses* strength over time. Further, repetitive activity tends to weaken motor nerve signals, and as a result, diminishes the power a muscle can generate. Likewise, soft connective tissues like fascia begin to form adhesions, which limits their stretching and "gliding" properties. Range of motion shrinks, and previous movement patterns can be altered.

Fitness planning can be categorized as "hard days" and "easy days." The hard days deliver stimulus needed to make gains, whereas the easier days enable the body to absorb the training. Without sufficient stimulus or harder days, fitness plateaus and eventually wanes; without easy days, the body ends up in a state of constant stress and cannot absorb training stimulus. In sum, some days need to be quite easy while others should be strenuous.

This offers the horse the spectrum needed, both mentally and physically, to make physiological adaptations. Many riders tend to spend too much time operating on one end of the spectrum, either accumulating large volumes of relatively easy work or pushing through hard workouts day after day. Neither of these scenarios results in sustainable strength gains.

A general rule of thumb for the weekly training sequence goes as follows: *easy, moderate, hard, repeat, rest*. In other words, your week might look like this example.

MONDAY
Easy. 35 to 50 minutes of light aerobic schooling, nothing mentally taxing or physically difficult.

TUESDAY
Moderate. 45 to 60 minutes of schooling including skills that are new or challenging to the horse.

WEDNESDAY
Hard. A good day to do a workout from this book.

THURSDAY
Easy. A repeat of Monday, or a 60-minute trail hack on mostly flat terrain.

FRIDAY
Moderate. Repeat Tuesday, or try a lower intensity workout from this book.

SATURDAY
Hard. A good day to do a long but low-intensity session (alternatively, do a shorter but more intense one). This can include a two-hour or longer trail ride, a double schooling session, or trailering out to a new location to school.

SUNDAY
Rest.

Duration and Intensity

Duration and *intensity* are the variables that determine whether a workout is hard or easy. The effort of any training session can be increased either by:

1. Making the session longer.
2. Increasing the intensity of exercises performed—that is, adding speed, power, or complexity to exercises.

To avoid negative stress and injury, do *not* increase both these variables at once. As you build fitness, you will strategically add *either* duration *or* intensity to certain workouts each week or two. Your specific goals and discipline will dictate which you choose, either duration or intensity, but just be sure to only turn up the dial on one at a time. In general, when duration increases and workouts become longer, they contain exercises performed at lower intensities. On the other hand, when exercises of greater intensity are called for, the work session is shorter with the horse in a "high-effort zone" for approximately 20 to 30 minutes or less, not including warm-up and cooldown.

Active Rest vs. Passive Rest

When building your weekly schedule, aim to avoid consecutive days of inactivity. Muscle cell metabolism suffers from multiple days off, resulting in subpar muscular contractions during the next session. Horses evolved to be in motion; this is how they thrive. Here is an example of when it is necessary to *not* anthropomorphize the horse's physiologic states. His well-being often does not improve with a day of sitting around in the same way we humans recharge. Rarely do horses benefit from numerous sedentary hours. When possible, try including *active rest* as part of days off as opposed to the horse just standing around.

As a broad rule, the horse's connective tissues, electrolytes and hormone balances, and muscle function benefit from the circulation of fluids brought on by light movement. To the contrary, inflammation and adhesions, soreness, and dysfunctional neuromuscular activity are worsened by time off that is sedentary. Obviously in the case of sickness or injury, a period of total inactivity would be appropriate. Otherwise, most

horses benefit from gentle activity on their days "off." For many riders, this involves reframing what it means to have a "rest" or "off day."

Active rest activity can take the form of a 30-minute hand-walk, an easy short trail ride, groundwork, or negotiating obstacles. The key is to keep efforts well below their usual working range. Active rest activities should steer clear of exercises from your everyday schooling routines. It should be viewed as a session of mentally and physically easy movement for the purpose of circulating fluids, fuels, and muscle enzymes.

Mobility Routines and Stretching

At some point most of us have considered using stretches from the ground to help our horses move with more ease, but we have likely wondered which ones to use and for how long. It is easy to get overwhelmed by the seemingly infinite number of stretches that exist, and yes, your horse might enjoy them all, but this does not mean he *needs* them all. If you plan a time-consuming pre- or post-ride routine, you are unlikely to stick with it. Unless your horse is in a prescribed rehab period, he will benefit greatly from just a couple of stretches after your rides throughout the week. On an average day, I do about three stretches for an individual horse; with extra time, I'll do up to five.

We need to make a distinction, however, between *mobilization* techniques versus *stretching* maneuvers. These two often get mixed up when riders are trying to figure out which beneficial things to do with their horses.

Mobility exercises use gentle motions to awaken and improve motion of one or more joints. They can help loosen areas of soft tissue that are stuck by stimulating the nerves around them and improving blood flow. Common examples include pelvic tucks, jaw flexions, belly lifts, or circling the forelimbs to loosen the shoulders. Through the gentle stimulation of mobility exercises, the body releases tension in targeted areas. Because such maneuvers also activate these richly innervated areas, the horse's sensory and motor nerves are better primed for full participation in the activities that follow. Mobility exercises can be performed any time but can be especially helpful *before*

2.1 Structured bouts of walking are an enormously beneficial way to add movement volume.

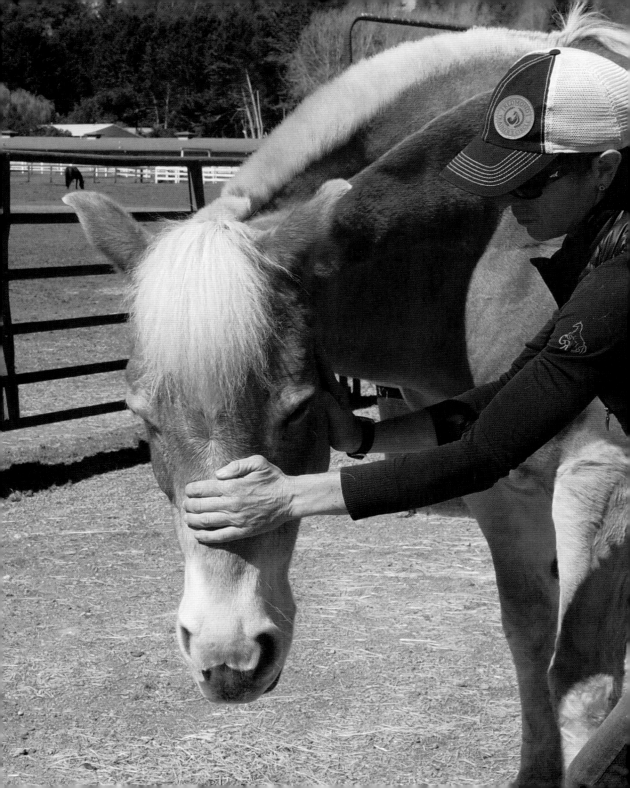

riding or training. Given that these exercises do not pull or stretch cold muscles, they are safe to do before warming up.

Active stretching, on the other hand, performed once the body is sufficiently warmed up, aims to loosen "stuck" areas by using physical manipulation or static traction. Popular stretches include pulling the horse's forelegs out in front of him or across his body. Once the muscles are oxygenated and warm, active stretching can help ensure fibers do not clump together. During these exercises, a muscle is stretched to the point of light resistance and then held in position for 10 to 20 seconds. They should be performed smoothly and non-forcefully. Otherwise, a muscle's *spindle receptors*, which protect from overstretching, will quickly contract the muscle to safeguard it. To be successful, stretches need to be undetected by these receptors, thus the importance of easing in and out of them, in addition to applying traction only to the point of light resistance.

In general, mobilization exercises should be performed for 10 to 20 seconds. The goal here is to send awakening signals to the nervous system; this happens with initial quick motions as opposed to a duration of activity that the horse can either tune out, brace against, or both. For active stretches, you want to hold each exercise for 20 to 30 seconds. Most studies agree that this is the timeframe required to create changes in the fascia and muscle cells. Obviously, if your horse seems to be really enjoying a particular maneuver and you have extra time, you can certainly go longer.

Through mobilization techniques and stretching, you can positively affect the horse's range of motion beyond what riding and groundwork exercises can accomplish. Additionally, you can guide the horse's nervous system to release tension and restriction. These exercises have cumulative results, however, and as with most principles relating to horses, consistency is key. If you wish for your horse to experience the benefits of stretching, you will need to commit to these drills at least three times weekly. In cases of excessive tension or physical rehab, it is necessary to perform stretching and mobility drills multiple times daily, at least five days per week.

The list of possible stretches can seem overwhelming; do not feel like you need to do every possible one with your horse every day. Choose three to five moves that seem

2.2 Before riding, I mobilize Arlington's poll. I use my hands to gently swivel his head from side to side, releasing poll tension.

relevant to your horse's needs. Every two weeks, switch to a new batch of exercises so that your horse's responses do not become muted by boring repetition. You do not *have* to do both mobilization and active stretching. If you have ample time, go ahead and do both, but remember when to do each one (mobilize *before* riding, stretch *afterward*).

When to "Double Up"

In terms of keeping a body primed for athletic activity, frequency and consistency of movement is paramount. For this reason, many successful conditioning plans employ *double sessions* a few days per week. By adding a second session to your horse's day occasionally, you can increase conditioning volume while minimizing boredom and fatigue and concussive forces that result from extending your regular training session. The general idea is that you add conditioning stimulus, allow the body to recover for a bit, and then add more conditioning. To be clear, the second session is intended to add light movement; it is NOT for the purpose of adding hard or strenuous work.

By using double sessions, you increase overall exercise volume throughout your horse's day, which is always more valuable than performing a stellar session but then having the horse stand around for the remaining 23 hours until his next one. Even excellent workouts don't pay off if the horse spends most of his day in a sedentary state. Many riders are accustomed to getting their horses out for a single focused effort of exercise daily, but some creative re-envisioning of the schedule can deliver heaps more movement, conditioning, and training results. In human fitness, we call this "greasing the groove" because we're optimizing the functionality of movement with multiple stimuli throughout the day rather than one exercise session followed by sitting around.

The specifics of each session in your double can differ considerably based on your horse's needs and level, but here I will offer basic guidelines, as well as real-life examples.

First, aim to conduct each session two to five hours apart. So far, research indicates that this timing allows your second session to build on your earlier conditioning effect. Each session can be the same length, although typically the second one is shorter. The minimum time I recommend is 15 minutes. In the instance of horses rehabbing from injury, the content of each double might be the same—for example, hand-walking and a few stretches or groundwork exercises. For performance horses in full training, the content of each might differ. Here is an example from my own barn:

A couple of times per week, I ride Diamante around 9:00 am, schooling his dressage movements in the arena for about 45 minutes. Then, I cool him down and put him in his paddock. After lunch around 1:00 pm, I get him back out for 20 minutes of groundwork, including brisk walking over ground poles and various corrective exercises (see sidebar). This second mini workout allows me to tune up his body mechanics, observe any tightness in his gaits, and keep his soft tissues hydrated, oxygenated, and adapting to the positive training stress we undertook in the morning. It also recirculates metabolic waste lingering in the tissues from the earlier workout, helping prevent stiffness or restriction.

For rehab cases, I try to employ multiple short sessions as often as possible. I aim for *at least* two sessions, sometimes three or four. These sessions range from 10 to 25 minutes. I find this always produces more effective results than a single session of hand-walking. Here is a sample schedule for a mare I am currently rehabbing:

At 7:45 am, when I arrive at the barn, I bring the mare to the arena and walk through ground pole routines and then perform several corrective exercises. After 20 minutes, she goes back to her paddock. Around noon, I bring her back out to perform a different batch of corrective exercises, totaling 10 or 15 minutes. And then before 2:00 pm, I get her out again to hand-walk on different surfaces and perform some stretches.

"Limbering Up" and "Warming Up"

In addition to muscle function that happens as a result of adequate blood and oxygen, proprioceptors need to be stimulated, neuromuscular patterns activated, and joint fluids lubricated. These changes happen during warm-ups,

"Corrective Exercises" Explained

"Corrective exercises" are maneuvers that target a horse's fine motor control and help keep his postural muscles activated. Performed with the right intention, numerous slow-moving exercises that require the horse to adjust his stride and posture without restrictive equipment serve this role. Examples include ground pole patterns, unmounted bending exercises, and variations of backing up. Advice on how to safely perform these, plus dozens of others, can be found in my book *55 Corrective Exercises for Horses*.

2.3 Diamante and I spend several minutes walking—both on a long rein and "in a frame"— before any training or fitness session.

and without them, workouts do not accomplish their goals. A good warm-up period should account for 20 percent of your total training time; it raises exercise intensity progressively so that the muscles increase temperature, oxygen supply, and pliability.

Warming up actually consists of two phases: an initial walking period followed by active warming up. At the beginning, horses need 8 to 12 minutes of uninterrupted walking to lubricate their joints prior to more vigorous exercise. This ensures the joint cartilage is not harmfully concussed and that proprioceptors are activated. In general, make a daily habit to walk on a long or loose rein for the first 10 minutes of a riding session.

For horses that live at pasture, it can be tempting to skip this part of the warm-up. But unless you are certain that the horse has spent the last 10 minutes in his field walking around continuously in a rhythmic and uninterrupted fashion as opposed to common turnout pastimes—napping, grazing, standing around—his joint fluids still require the walking phase. Beyond joint health, this initial period is also crucial for ensuring the horse's postural and stabilizing muscles are properly activated. During this period of gentle movement, the horse's sensory and motor nerves gradually increase their activity. As a result, the muscles that are responsible for stability and fine motor control during movement can be accessed. This is akin to having "all the circuits functioning" that are responsible for communication with the entire musculoskeletal system. When warm-ups are rushed or cut short, however, the horse's proprioception is not fully awakened. As a result, the larger locomotive muscles take over the roles of movement *and* stabilizing and postural adjustments. They are not suited for these latter roles, which means their overactivation creates poor movement patterns. The body soon becomes habituated to dysfunctional ways of moving.

After the critical initial period of walking, the body then needs a lively warm up. This can last 10 to 15 minutes beyond the walking phase and includes activities that are energetic enough to push blood and oxygen into the muscles as well as increase their temperature for pliability. A productive warm-up, therefore, involves more than just wandering around for a set amount of time. Typically, it includes lively trotting and cantering, plus a series of gait transitions while performing a variety of patterns to introduce lateral bending and engagement of the horse's hind legs.

In general, harder workouts require more vigorous warm-ups to prepare the body, whereas easier ones can rely on simpler, shorter warm-ups. Bear this in mind as you work through this book. For instance, if you are going to do The 4x3 gallop set workout (p. 81), be sure to engage in a very active warm-up that includes brisk trotting and cantering, plus transitions and speed changes in each gait, before tackling the workout. On the other hand, if you plan to do one of the Groundwork Routines (Workouts 1 through 14—p. 40), a period of walking plus some mobility drills will suffice.

The workouts in chapters 4 and 5 do not prescribe specific warm-ups, but they *do* assume that a warm-up will be conducted beforehand. It will be up to you as the rider to craft sufficient warm-ups for each workout by following the guidelines I have provided. Depending on a given horse's age, fitness, and training trajectory, overall exercise duration can be increased by lengthening warm-up and cooldown periods. Follow the workouts as they are presented, but feel free to extend pre- and post-exercise by a few minutes, so long as it is low intensity and not tedious. In other words, extra volume should include relatively easy and straightforward movement, not nit-picking schooling or high aerobic efforts.

PART TWO:
EXERCISE QUICK REFERENCE

3

The Key Exercises

In this section, I describe the key exercises that factor prominently through-out the following chapters.

EQUIPMENT:

- Halter, lead rope, and longe line (I prefer a cavesson with a center ring on the noseband—see p. 45 for an easy tip for recreating this on your regular halter.)
- A long whip to extend your reach (dressage, longe, or driving)
- Elevated platform (see options for alternatives)
- Cavalletti risers (or alternatives—be creative!)
- 3 to 5 cones
- 6 to 8 ground poles
- For mounted exercises, the basic tack you regularly school in.

Back-Up

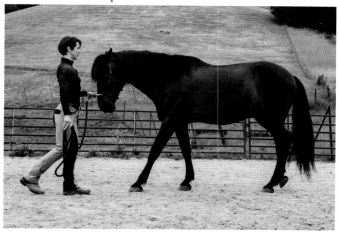

3.1 I ask Corazon to back up with straight rhythmic steps while also asking him to lower his neck slightly. With the rope and cavesson, I lightly draw his neck out and down while my body language—stepping toward him—tells him to back up. If he becomes crooked as he steps, I ask him to slow down or stop before proceeding.

UNMOUNTED

1. Many of the fitness routines require you to back your horse up a prescribed number of steps from the ground. Each foreleg stepping back counts as a single step.
2. As you ask for the back-up, aim to keep the horse's neck level with his torso, neither too high nor too low.

MOUNTED

1. There are many varying cues and preferences amongst riders for backing a horse up from the saddle. In the absence of your own preferences, however, begin at a quiet standstill, adjusting your reins to establish a light feeling of both corners of the horse's mouth.

A Word About Ground Poles

There are no such things as "perfect" ground poles. For fitness purposes, a variety of materials and lengths can be used, from wooden ground poles to actual logs to landscaping timbers to fence posts or tree branches. My advice is always to use the simplest option available to you. If you have random posts of varying lengths hanging around your property, they can work fine. Too many students miss out on the value of exercises like those I share in these pages because they lack access to the "fancy poles" seen in equestrian magazines. You do not need long or painted poles. Find options, preferably wood that does not shatter in cold temperatures like plastic does, that will not wrench your back to move around and that you are likely to use on a regular basis.

2. Keep your legs gently closed around the horse's ribcage to convey that you're about to ask him to move his feet.

3. Draw your upper body slightly backward while simultaneously closing your fingers on the reins, but do not pull the reins back. The horse will follow your body language and energy by stepping backward.

TIP: Aim for smooth and *straight* steps backward, not drifting to one side.

Step-Ups

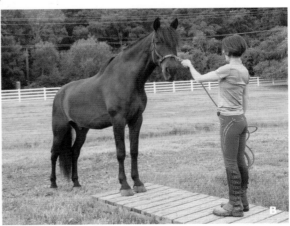

3.2 A & B Corazon prepares to step his forefeet on the platform (A). After he steps his front feet on the platform, I ask him to step back down (B), usually, after one or two seconds' pause—unless it appears (yawning, lowered eyelids, licking) the horse is experiencing a big release, in which case I wait 10 or more seconds before having him step down.

1. Stand with your horse facing a block or platform that is 8 inches high or taller. In most cases, I find it helps for the handler to stand on the platform and guide the horse straight toward her. In cases where the horse seems apprehensive, it will be better to stand beside the horse's shoulder and step up onto the platform, encouraging the horse to mimic you.

2. Ask the horse to step his front feet on top of the platform.

3. Then, ask him to step them back down to the ground. Keep the horse's feet close to the platform in order to immediately begin the next rep. Try not to "fade away" from the block.
4. Repeat this sequence a designated number of times.

TIP: In the absence of a suitable platform, alternatives include the back of a horse trailer, a ramp, or a step up to an elevated barn aisle. Maintain straight alignment through the horse's body, no drifting askew with the haunches.

Step-Downs

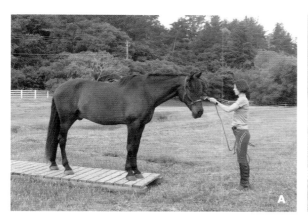 

3.3 A & B Corazon prepares to step just his front feet down off the platform (A). Now I ask Corazon to step his front feet back up on the platform (B).

1. Begin by standing your horse quietly on a platform measuring 8 inches or taller.
2. Step just the horse's front feet down to the ground.
3. Now ask the horse to back up, stepping back up onto the platform with his front feet, and resume his starting position.
4. Repeat this sequence a designated number of times.

TIP: Note the platform alternatives from the previous exercise can apply here, as well. If your platform is quite tall, you may modify the exercise by asking the horse to take small steps forward and backward with his front feet remaining on the ground, hind feet on the platform.

Up-and-Overs

3.4 A & B Corazon approaches the platform with smooth rhythm (A). He steps up and over the platform for the designated number of reps in our workout (B). His neck and topline are visibly relaxed and he is taking big, full steps with his hind legs.

1. Lead or longe your horse calmly at a walk only over a raised platform measuring 8 inches or taller.
2. Maintain a smooth, steady rhythm while approaching and crossing the platform.
3. Repeat for prescribed time, changing directions halfway through.

TIP: In the absence of a suitable platform, alternatives that can often be used for this exercise include ramps, berms or dirt piles, or bridges.

Lateral Yields

3.5 A & B In a lateral yield from the ground, I ask Corazon to move his body forward and sideways away from me by stepping toward his shoulder, my body language telling him to yield sideways with his line of travel (A). He crosses his front and hind legs in a walking rhythm (B). If he exaggerates the sideways motion, I will use my hand on the rope to draw him straight forward momentarily.

UNMOUNTED

1. Position yourself at your horse's shoulder, facing it.
2. Now ask the horse to step away from you, moving his body sideways and slightly forward with each step.
3. You are looking for both front and hind legs to cross over as the horse continues to step sideways.

MOUNTED

1. From a working walk with light rein contact, ask your horse to swivel his head slightly to the left by gently turning your left wrist and drawing your left shoulder back. Maintain steady walk rhythm.

2. Apply on-off pressure with your left leg positioned at the girth, asking your horse to step sideways-and-forward with each stride. The horse should move in a diagonal line of travel to the right.

3. Reverse the instructions in Steps 1 and 2 to perform a lateral yield in the opposite direction.

Turn-on-the-Forehand

3.6 I ask Corazon's front feet to remain stationary while his hind legs step around them in the turn-on-the-forehand. Note here his right hind leg steps across his left.

1. Stand in front of your horse, facing him at a standstill.

2. Ask for slight lateral poll flexion to the right; then immediately direct your gaze and whip (if you are carrying one) toward his right flank.

3. Ask the horse's hindquarters to move away from this request. His right hind leg should cross repeatedly in front of this left, forming an "X" if viewed from behind.

4. The horse's forefeet remain in place but can step up and down on the spot.
5. Continue moving the hindquarters around in a full 360-degree revolution.
6. Repeat the same sequence of steps on the horse's left side.

TIP: As the horse turns, be sure the neck stays aligned in front of the horse's trunk as opposed to bending around toward the sideways-stepping leg. Pause as needed to reset, especially if you encounter a lot of resistance from your horse.

Turn-on-the-Haunches

3.7 A & B I ask Corazon's forehand to yield away from me while his back legs remain stationary in the turn-on-the-haunches (A). You can see the left front leg has stepped across the right as I asked (B).

1. Stand facing your horse's left shoulder. He should be immobile and standing straight.
2. Step toward the horse with upright body language, and if needed, a light cue from the whip directed at his shoulder.
3. Ask the horse's front end to step sideways away from you. His hind feet should remain in place, not stepping forward.

4. Continue asking his front end to step sideways until you have completed a 180-degree turn. (Typically, it is more difficult to keep proper form in the Turn-on-the-Haunches versus the Turn-on-the-Forehand. It requires more coordination and stability from the horse. Certainly, when a horse is very experienced at Turn-on-the-Haunches, a 360-degree turn can be done. For others, a 180-degree turn is suitable and effective.)

5. Repeat on the right side.

TIP: Ideally, in this exercise the horse bends in the direction of the turn. This means, the poll and neck will bend slightly away from you. If the horse routinely steps back with his hind feet, it can help to position him against a fence while also positioning yourself a bit more in front of the horse.

Tight Serpentine

3.8 A & B In the tight serpentine exercise, I prepare Corazon to switch from bending left to bending right without losing the rhythm of his walk (A). Now I ask him to bend his body to the right for three strides before bending back to the left (B).

1. Stand directly in front of your horse with your rope in your right hand and a long whip (such as a longe whip with the lash secured) in your left.

2. Begin by walking straight backward and drawing the horse toward you.

3. Use your whip directed at his rib cage on one side to ask him to bend his body around it. Proceed three strides like this.

4. Now, reach across with your whip to the opposite side of his ribcage and ask for a bend in this new direction.

5. Repeat this sequence, asking the horse to walk in a steady rhythm and change his bend every three strides.

TIP: It is imperative to maintain a smooth, steady rhythm while changing bends in this exercise. This happens from the handler walking with clear purpose to guide the horse.

Pre-Ride Circles

3.9 While walking backward on a small circle around a cone, I use my whip to encourage Corazon's inside hind leg to step slightly to the inside of the hoofprint left by his forefoot. Often directing his attention in this way is enough, but if needed, I can reach back and touch his thigh or hind cannon bone with the whip to clarify. My hand on the rope applies light traction to invite his neck to reach out and downward.

1. Walk backward as you guide the horse in a 6-meter circle around a cone.

2. Invite the horse's neck to stretch as low to the ground as possible while bending toward the cone. Do this by applying gentle traction down and outward with your leading hand, as if you're drawing the horse's muzzle toward your own knees. Do not force this stretch; just make a suggestion.

Raised Uneven Poles

3.10 A & B Alternating raised ends of the ground poles offer a valuable visual and physical stimulus.

1. Set up six parallel poles spaced approximately 2½ feet apart with alternating ends raised to a height of 8 inches.
2. Walk alongside your horse over the poles, or longe him at a walk over the poles. Your position should be dictated by the best option to help your horse travel straight—not arced or crooked—over each pole.

TIP: Creative materials can be used to raise the poles if you do not have cavalletti risers. The height that you raise alternating ends of the poles is also flexible: 8 inches is a good general guideline, but it can be higher or slightly lower, depending on your available supplies and your horse's abilities and needs.

Clockface Poles

1. On a 20-meter circle (or larger), place two parallel poles at each quarter mark; space them approximately 4 feet apart at their centers, and raise them 6 to 8 inches high.
2. The inside ends of the poles can be closer together, the outer ends can be slightly wider.
3. Longe your horse at a trot, crossing all eight poles. Repeat for the number of times prescribed.

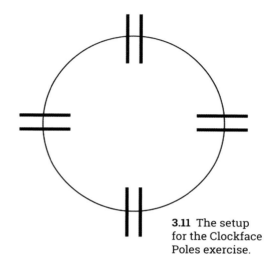

3.11 The setup for the Clockface Poles exercise.

Wide Poles

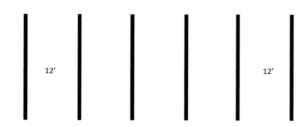

3.12 The setup for the Wide Poles exercise.

1. Place six parallel poles in a sequence, spaced 12 feet apart from each other and raised to a height of 6 inches.
2. Ride across or between the poles, or a combination of both.

TIP: Be sure the area around the poles is clear of objects or holes; do not set up this exercise near a fence or wall.

Agile Athlete

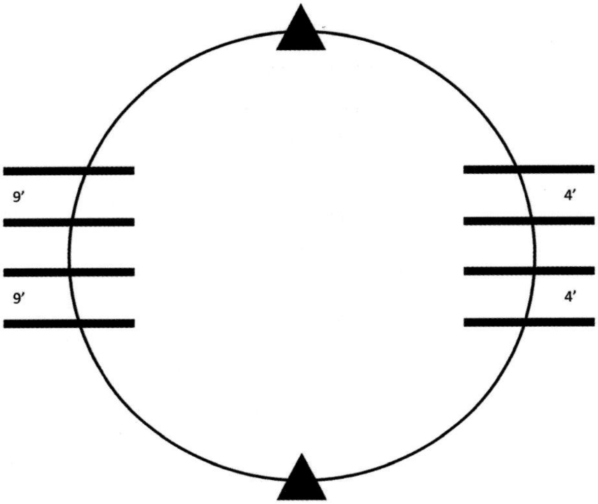

1. On one side of a large circle, set up four parallel poles that measure 9 feet apart at their centers. Position the inside ends slightly closer and outside ends slightly wider. This allows you to choose a line of travel over the poles that best accommodates your horse's canter stride length. Raise poles to a height of 6 to 8 inches.

3.13 The setup for the Agile Athlete exercise.

2. On the opposite side of the large circle, set up four parallel poles that measure 4 feet apart at their centers and slightly wider at their outer edges. These poles can either be raised or lying flat on the ground.

3. It also helps to place cones at the other two sides of your circle as shown in the diagram.

4. The objective is to ride your horse at a canter over the first set of poles, adjusting your line of travel toward the outside or inside edge of the poles to accommodate the horse's length of stride. You want to land neatly in the middle of each set of poles and immediately bound over the next pole without losing the rhythm of the canter.

5. Approaching the first cone (at the top of the circle in the diagram), transition downward to trot and proceed over the second set of poles.

6. Approaching the second cone (at the bottom of the circle in the diagram), resume cantering and continue over the four canter poles.

7. Repeat the prescribed number of times in both directions.

PART THREE:
WORKOUTS AND SCHEDULES FOR STRENGTH AND FITNESS

4

Groundwork Routines (Secret Conditioning)

While it is widely used for gentling young horses and teaching basic skills, groundwork also offers the possibility for a notable amount of conditioning. When consistently and strategically practiced, it can improve muscle tone, basic metabolic function, and neuromuscular patterns. Increasingly, evidence has shown that a large percentage of muscle activity can be maintained in non-ridden horses when groundwork sessions are performed six or more times per week.

Groundwork for Fitness vs. Groundwork for Training

The key to groundwork success is its consistency. When practiced sporadically, physical gains will not be made, although it could arguably still benefit the horse's mental state. Purpose and structure in your sessions matters a lot, too. Many horse owners fall in a rut of doing the same games, obstacles, or maneuvers with their horse either to achieve relaxation or bonding. These can still be a fun way to spend time, but when fitness is sought, these routines need to be adapted to include the necessary dosages of novel stimulus, intervals, and progressive challenges.

Fitness-based groundwork differs from other ground training for horses in several ways. These workouts are aimed at activating and exercising the body to make conditioning gains. They will be most successful when a horse already possesses certain basics, including:

1. Solid ground manners.
2. Yielding sideways when cued.
3. Halting promptly.
4. Moving in rhythm alongside the handler.

These routines do not seek to teach or refine specific skills so much as give the horse's body opportunities to become more athletic. Namely, through fitness-based groundwork we can contribute to a horse's athleticism in the following ways:

- Improve neuromuscular activation and coordination.
- Increase activity of sensory and motor nerves.
- Awaken poorly recruited muscles.
- Strengthen postural muscle and ligament system.
- Introduce relaxation and positive feeling during physical efforts (a crucial cornerstone of future athletic progress).
- Gain balance, alignment, joint flexion, and rhythm of gaits.
- Introduce or maintain a baseline muscular tone and metabolic condition during periods of less or limited ridden work.

Fitness-based groundwork differs significantly from longeing or repetitive circling. In fact, it aims to perform circles sparingly, carefully, and with purpose. Due to the unevenness of ground reaction forces (GRF)—the force exerted by the ground on a body in contact with it—on the horse's limbs when circling, repetition leads to asymmetry in the horse's back muscles, not to mention the potential stress to hoof structures. Given that our goal is to improve, rather than detract from, the horse's locomotion, the use of circles is judicious. Moreover, the locomotion while circling is varied throughout sessions (gaits, speeds, changes of direction). In order to avoid excessive

4.1 Unless circles are specifically prescribed, do your best to walk and jog alongside your horse on straight and open lines of travel.

circling, successful groundwork routines rely on handlers willing to move around and cover a fair amount of ground each session.

Be prepared to move a lot. This allows the horse to change his line of travel frequently, triggering the postural adjustments that make the routines in this chapter productive. If this amount of mobility challenges you, find a helper who can perhaps fulfill the non-technical intervals (walking and jogging straight lines) of the session between exercise reps.

Groundwork workouts also avoid prolonged pauses, aiming to keep the horse's body mostly in motion. Additionally, they utilize specific time intervals and sequencing of maneuvers to make the best physiological adaptations. The duration of each workout is based on optimal standards for creating meaningful stimulus, so it is important to follow the prescriptions I provide in the following pages. If you have a pre-existing set of skills-based groundwork, games, or obstacles you enjoy doing with your horse,

The Basics of Equine Heart Rate

An average horse has a resting heart rate between 30 and 40 *beats per minute* or *bpm* (see page 75 for more about how to determine this). Depending on breed, age, and fitness, most horses have a maximum upper limit of 200 bpm after which point they enter very taxing metabolic territory. Most performance horses doing light work (walking, jogging on flat ground) measure between 100 to 130 bpm. Their heart rates during moderate work (trotting and cantering, ascending hills, jumping) range from 140 bpm to 170 bpm.

Again, the specifics of heart rate depend on genetic and individual factors, and while it is not entirely necessary for most riders to use a heart rate monitor, I do often recommend them. By no means will you use one daily or even weekly, but taking a reading of your horse's heart rate during work (rather than at a standstill, which is the only way you can take it manually) at least every couple of months will give you an accurate, non-subjective data point. This data point can indicate if/when fitness has progressed, declined, or is perhaps affected by stress and anxiety. Heart rate monitoring also becomes incredibly valuable over the course of a horse's lifetime when determining if a senior horse is still capable of activities that have been easy for him in the past.

they can be incorporated *after* the fitness workout, assuming their intensity level is complementary.

Exercise sports studies have shown that in order to prevent *fitness erosion*, a horse needs to perform *a minimum* of 25 minutes of exercise with his heart rate at 40 percent or higher than his usual maximum. For most horses, this means spending 25 minutes or longer at a low aerobic rate of 90 to 100 beats per minute, or in other words, a brisk walk or slow jog. The following routines follow this baseline parameter.

Equipment to Use...and Not to Use

A little preparation will ensure that you reap the most benefits from your groundwork routine. First, any "training aids" that restrict the horse's head or neck mobility (side-reins, longeing equipment) are not recommended. It is also not recommended to attach your lead rope or line to the horse's bit. The horse's jaw, tongue, and sensitive mouth structures should remain free from and unimpeded by signals or pressure during these workouts, allowing topline and underside muscle chains to fully release tension on their own. I find the best option is a longe cavesson or a flat halter that fits well (that is, it is not so loose that it twists around the horse's face), and that allows you to guide the horse with a light amount of tension *without* twisting the horse's nose toward you.

Lacking access to a longe cavesson, you can use a 6-inch loop of sturdy rope (like paracord) and fasten it in a *prusik knot* around the noseband of a halter. The prusik knot is a "slide-and-grip knot," which means that when it isn't weighted, it slides easily, but when pulled, it grips tightly. Tying this knot involves wrapping a loop a few times inwardly around the noseband and then tightening the knot as shown in the diagram in Figure 4.2 A.

The length and material of your rope or line can vary. This is a matter of personal preference. Handlers usually operate most effectively without excess rope getting tangled around their feet, so a good general guideline is to use a 20-foot rope. This can be altered based on the size of your horse and your personal preference. Note that most modern longe lines are not ideal for groundwork as they are not only too flat and wide in your hand but they are also lightweight, making them unstable to hold as you move around. A better option is one that sits with more weight in your palm and is shaped like a snake. Over the years my own preference has been gently used ropes from the local climbing gym; others rely on the kind of ropes used for sailing. There are lots of options, but basically you want a line that "sinks down" in your palm with some weight and does not fill up your entire hand.

Use What You Have

Where certain equipment is required, feel free to use creativity. In the absence of ground poles, for instance, many students have improvised with logs, planks, and even smooth tree branches. In the absence of proper hills, modifications can be made so that ditches,

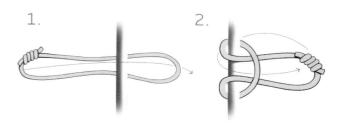

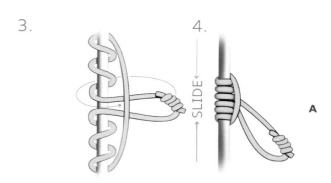

4.2 A-C To tie a prusik knot (A): 1) Wrap a loop of cord around the noseband of your halter. 2) Then, pass the loop back through the loop itself. 3) Do this three or four more times until excess cord is used up. 4) Squeeze the two ends of the knot together. Attach your lead rope to the loop of cord that remains (here reinforced with black tape—B), creating a makeshift longeing cavesson (C).

ramps, berms, or driveways serve the necessary purpose. I have seen students devise wonderful and creative solutions when they lacked the specified equipment. Bear in mind that the purpose of these workouts is the stimulus they offer the horse. Often this stimulus can be replicated in several ways, even if you lack access to a wide array of tools or terrain. You can still make conditioning gains, even without the perfect setting or apparatus. Fitness comes from *consistency* of exercise more than perfection of facilities or weather. Most of the following workouts can also be done without an arena. In most cases, a paddock or reasonably flat open area will suffice.

Success Story

On New Year's Day in 2023, a catastrophic storm hit our county. Rivers flooded, roads collapsed, redwood trees fell over and ripped apart hillsides. At our property, the horses stood in water over their hooves for days as we desperately waited for the creeks to recede. Unbeknownst to us, the following three months would bring twelve more of these powerful storms. The winter of 2023 was relentless and destructive. It forced 6,000 people to evacuate their homes, took the lives of 22 individuals, and forced numerous businesses to shut. Day after day brought more rain and mud and wind.

Here on California's central coast, our climate is normally very mild year-round. It is so mild, in fact, that most of us do not have covered arenas or, for that matter, barns. We keep our horses outside and train outdoors because the elements are typically pleasant…until last winter. As rain poured down on me every day and my arena became a mud pit, I could only rely on groundwork for the 10 horses at my barn. Days became weeks and then months. For three months, I could do little more than daily groundwork while wearing many layers of rain gear and rubber boots. I followed routines like the ones here in this book

Workout Prep

Many of the following workouts call for some work with ground poles (see p. 27), varied surfaces, a step-up platform, or a hillside. Success depends on moving without interruption between each exercise circuit, which means having your "tasks" set up ahead of time and being prepared to shift from one to the next. Have your poles already laid out, any necessary gates open, and lines of travel unobstructed.

It also helps to read through each routine ahead of time and have a general sense of what you will be doing. Once you begin the workout, try to avoid pauses. The goal is to

and while I longed for my normal riding and training routines, I trusted these sessions to work. Especially for the few senior horses at our barn, I wanted to avoid big losses of strength and fitness.

I can report that we did just fine! When winter finally passed, the horses had all maintained their baseline fitness, thanks to all that rain-soaked groundwork, and we resumed our regular riding. By the time our arena and hills dried out enough for riding workouts, the horses did not feel like they had missed any training despite that very long, challenging winter. My local colleagues, meanwhile, needed to spend most of the spring re-conditioning their horses or dealing with the kinds

of unsoundness or behavioral problems that arise with extensive inactivity.

Even though I had to get creative and find areas to use for groundwork *and* learn to tolerate wet feet and cold hands, I managed to complete 25 to 30 minutes of productive movement with my horses daily. Many days this meant timed walks up and down the paved driveway, moving my ground poles to a paddock with higher ground, performing Lateral Yields, Turn-on-the-Haunches, and controlled periods of slow jogging in the muddy round pen. I used a former grooming platform for Step-Ups and Step-Downs. On days I was certain the road was not washing away, we headed out on 2-mile hikes.

Follow Timelines

At least when initially practicing these groundwork workouts, use a timing device. The interval durations should be followed closely, and many factors can make a certain task "feel" longer or shorter than it should be, especially prolonged bouts of walking. To ensure the right stimulus, time yourself with a clock. Do not try to guess based on feel.

keep the horse "in the effort" for the prescribed time. When the handler needs to stop frequently to consult instructions, it negates this momentum. Depending on the duration of each pause, accumulated downtime can override the physical benefit of each session.

Daily Doses

Unlike the more intense workouts of chapters 5 and 6 (pp. 72 and 88), these groundwork fitness routines can be practiced daily. That is not to say you should practice the *same* one day after day, but you can mix and match throughout the week. When used this way, I have known numerous horses that managed to maintain—and in some cases *improve*—their fitness during periods of no riding. Especially in the cases of inclement weather, physical rehab, or periods of downtime, these routines are immensely helpful. When relying on groundwork only, it becomes especially important to ensure the horse receives four to six sessions per week. You will notice these are not time-intensive—many last only about 25 minutes—but the consistency of stimulus prevents the body from "de-training" (according to the National Institutes of Health, this is the "the partial or complete loss of training-induced adaptations, in response to an insufficient training stimulus").

Aside from being a stand-alone session in the instances noted on page 49, these low-intensity sessions can be used on *active rest days* or as a warm-up for one of your riding days. When using groundwork routines as a warm-up, perform just the first 15 minutes of the routine, and then carry on with the rest of your plan for the day, which might include a lesson, schooling session, or trail ride.

Choose the Right Workout

The following workouts offer a wide variety of difficulty levels. Many include exercises performed primarily at walk with only short intervals of more challenging tasks, while others include sustained trotting or cantering sequences. This allows you to choose workouts appropriate for your individual horse. If you seek workouts to use during inclement weather, rehabilitation phases, or senior years, you will find plenty of predominantly walk-based workouts appropriate for your horse. On the other hand, if you wish to increase fitness gains during periods of consistent training but no riding, choose from the more active options.

Injuries, Recovery, and Chronic Weakness

Many of you will find your way to this chapter while trying to solve a persistent gait dysfunction or navigate post-injury exercise protocol. To this end, I would like to offer the following guidance to help you along. Remember that these are very *general* recommendations, and your ideal scenario will include consulting your vet, therapists, and local support team.

At Least Six Weeks

Where strength is concerned, it often takes six weeks to see the results of any new routine or exercise protocol. Keep this in mind as you proceed, since many days it might seem like you are not advancing. To determine if a particular set of exercises is working for your horse, you *must* allow enough time. There is no way to shortcut physiology. Many of us are too quick to decide a routine is not working after just a few days. The body does not make strength gains this quickly. While there will likely be intermittent indications along the way whether a routine is—or is not—working, a full and accurate assessment should not be made before six weeks.

Begin Stationary

A post-injury conditioning plan should begin with two weeks of stationary exercises, which can often begin *while* the horse is still recuperating from injury. The specifics of these exercises will vary depending on the injury, but common examples include dynamic mobilization of limbs and spine, pelvic tucks, triggering reflexes, and bodywork maneuvers. At this stage, the horse benefits most from *frequency* of these exercises as opposed to duration of each. In other words, it is optimal to perform your prescribed stationary exercises five or six times, spaced throughout each day.

Frequency Over Duration

Once the horse is cleared to begin controlled exercise, continue adhering to this principle of frequency for the initial two weeks. For example, if your vet recommends walking the horse for a set amount of time daily, ask how many sessions per day this figure can be divided into. Frequency of neuromuscular activity is the goal.

Progressive Challenge Is Key

After two weeks of *controlled exercise*, primarily in the form of hand-walking, most horses will be able to do many of the routines in this chapter. Again, depending on the injury, not all of them will be suitable. But many can be performed as-is or in a modified form in order to continue reconditioning in a more productive and holistic fashion than longeing in circles or hand-walking up and down the driveway ad nauseam.

Here is where reconditioning plans get tricky. Out of fear of reinjuring the horse, or due to a lack of a clear prescription from a vet, owners can get stuck in this controlled exercise phase. In order to be effective, exercise plans need to be *progressively challenging*. Unless there is clear evidence to suggest otherwise, the plan needs to continue increasing duration of sessions and novelty of exercises.

Remember, the goals of a rehab period are to:

1. Remove pain.
2. Restore or improve range of motion.
3. Restore or improve strength and overall fitness of the horse.

A successful plan does not end after completing Step 2, though we may breathe a sigh of relief when the pain seems resolved and the horse is moving well.

As the horse regains a normal riding routine and all is going consistently well for those initial few weeks, the routines in chapters 5 and 6 become critical. They help increase the horse's musculoskeletal fitness, which serves a protective role from reinjury. To reiterate, when a horse is kept too long in a repetitive state of low-effort work due to an owner's fear of injury repercussion, his body is *more* susceptible to failure, not less. The horse *does* need increasingly harder efforts.

Success Story

Last year, the owner of a lovely gelding named Eli wrote to me looking for a plan that might help him. Unfortunately, Eli had been diagnosed with Lyme disease shortly after his owner bought him. In addition to becoming reactive, Eli developed challenges with body control and expressions of discomfort, like foot stomping, agitation, nipping, and neck and topline rigidity. Along with her trainer, Eli's owner spent several months rehabilitating him and wondering if he would ever return to being the promising dressage horse that initially arrived at the barn.

Based on the work they had already done, I wrote a four-week conditioning plan of low-intensity routines that would hopefully bring Eli to the point of resuming a normal volume of riding. His plan included five days per week, combining both groundwork and light riding, mostly walking. The groundwork routines relied extensively on Raised Uneven Poles (p. 36), Tight Serpentines (p. 34), Back-Up (p. 27), and measured periods of sustained movement in addition to mobility exercises before each session. Two days per week, I suggested Eli perform a second shorter session in the afternoon following the morning routine. This gave Eli a greater frequency of movement, a necessary part of retraining neuromotor patterns, while keeping his overall schedule low impact. I also hoped, in Eli's case, that distributing workload over multiple brief sessions would minimize tension and keep him more mentally engaged with tasks. It allowed us to add exercise volume without the possible deleterious results of lengthening individual workouts.

Eli's dressage trainer helped oversee the plan, and while the quality of his movement wavered slightly from day to day, the overall progress trajectory was forward. I was thrilled to receive an email from his owner near the end of the plan, where she said: "I cannot tell you the difference this program has made in Eli! I finally feel like I have the horse I bought two years ago! It is not perfect, but I now feel like he is working with me. My instructor is thrilled."

WORKOUT 1
Step-Ups and Transitions

4.3 A-D Step-Ups (A), Step-Downs (B), Up-and-Overs (C), and Lateral Yields (C).

DURATION: Approximately 25 minutes

KEY EXERCISES USED: Step-Ups (p. 28), Step-Downs (p. 29), Up-and-Overs (p. 30), Lateral Yields (p. 31)

BENEFITS: This workout is terrific for releasing tension in the horse's shoulders while improving coordination. It is useful during times of poor weather or an active rest day. While the movements are meant to flow continuously, you can allow brief pauses when the horse shows signs of significant tension release (chewing, sighing, eyelid twitch) during the Step-Ups. Allow the release to happen and then carry on.

HOW-TO:

1. For 10 minutes: Walk at brisk pace without stopping.
2. For 2 minutes: Walk 10 steps, stop, back up 6 steps; repeat sequence.
3. For 3 minutes: Walk-to-jog transitions (every 10 steps). *Ideally, jog alongside your horse on mostly straight lines.*
4. Do 10 reps of Step-Ups.
5. For 2 minutes: Repeat Step 3.
6. Do 10 reps of Step-Downs.
7. Do 10 reps of Up-and-Overs.
8. For 1 minute: Walk at brisk pace.
9. For 45-seconds: Do Lateral Yields in each direction. Repeat twice.
10. Finish by performing any stretches you wish, or five minutes of easy jogging.

WORKOUT 2

Mobility Magic

DURATION: Approximately 35 minutes
KEY EXERCISES USED: Back-Up (p. 27), Turn-on-the-Forehand (p. 32), Turn-on-the-Haunches (p. 33), Tight Serpentines (p. 34)
BENEFITS: This session can be performed pretty much anywhere with moderately level ground. It can help loosen areas where horses often hold tension. These gentle maneuvers can activate the *postural muscle system* (sensory pathways that transmit information to the central nervous system, thus controlling posture).

HOW-TO:

1. For 10 minutes: Walk, making speed changes every 15 strides (slow, medium, very fast).
2. Back the horse up 30 steps.
3. For 2 minutes: Walk-to-stop transitions (every 10 steps); repeat.
4. Turn-on-the-Forehand 3 times in each direction.
5. For 2 minutes: Easy jog on straight lines and big circles.
6. Turn-on-the-Haunches 3 times in each direction.

4.4 A-D Back-Up (A), Turn-on-the-Forehand (B), Turn-on-the-Haunches (p. C), and Tight Serpentines (D).

7. For 2 minutes: Walk briskly.
8. Repeat Steps 4 through 6.
9. For 2 minutes: Walk Tight Serpentines.
10. For 30 seconds: Lateral Yield in each direction. Repeat twice.
11. Finish with your favorite stretches, liberty play, or turnout for extra movement.

TIP: Aim to perform a full 360-degree turn unless your horse is just learning, healing from a lower limb or hoof injury, or particularly stiff, in which case perform a 180-degree turn.

WORKOUT 3
Basics for Breakfast

4.5 A-D Pre-Ride Circles (A), Raised Uneven Poles (B), Back-Up (C), and Tight Serpentines (D).

DURATION: Approximately 25 minutes

KEY EXERCISES USED: Pre-Ride Circles (p. 35), Raised Uneven Poles (p. 36), Back-Up (p. 27), Tight Serpentines (p. 34)

BENEFITS: Combining different lines of travel, transitions, *and* ground poles, this simple routine is one to revisit frequently. Be sure to have your ground poles set up ahead of time; you can perform reps either by setting up poles on one side of a large longe circle or by hand-walking back and forth across them. Choose the longe option if you have extra time; your horse spends more time walking with this one.

HOW-TO:

1. For 3 minutes: Perform Pre-Ride Circles continuously, alternating each direction.
2. Walk over Raised Uneven Poles for 20 reps.
3. For 3 minutes: Walk Tight Serpentines.
4. For 4 minutes: Walk-to-jog transitions (every 20 steps). *Ideally, jog alongside your horse on mostly straight lines.*
5. Repeat Raised Uneven Poles for 10 reps.
6. For 3 minutes: Walk 20 steps, stop, back up 6 to 8 steps; repeat sequence.
7. Finish with 5 minutes of easy jogging.

TIP: Be sure you do not tilt the horse's head toward you when crossing ground poles. We want the horse's head and neck to remain very straight over poles.

WORKOUT 4

Round Pen Ramblin'

DURATION: Approximately 35 minutes

KEY EXERCISES USED: Pre-Ride Circles (p. 35), Lateral Yield (p. 31), Turn-on-the-Haunches (p. 33)

BENEFITS: If you only have a small space to train in, like a round pen, it becomes even more necessary to avoid repetition and concussive forces when working with

4.6 A-D Pre-Ride Circles (A), Lateral Yields (B), Turn-on-the-Haunches (C), and leaving the round pen to walk straight lines (D).

your horse. There *is* productive work to be done in a round pen, but it requires diligent distribution of exercises within a session. By relying on a variety of stimuli, this work-out—and the two that follow—are beneficial without being unduly repetitive.

HOW-TO:

1. For 10 minutes: Walk, making speed changes every 15 strides (slow, medium, very fast). Do this on straight lines, using your driveway, paddocks, or a field. Then proceed to the round pen.
2. For 2 minutes: Pre-Ride Circles in both directions.
3. For 3 minutes (each direction): Slow jog around the perimeter of the pen.
4. Lateral Yield half-way around the pen in each direction.
5. For 2 minutes (each direction): Brisk trot around the perimeter.
6. Turn-on-the-Haunches 180 degrees, 3 times in each direction. After each turn, walk forward a few steps.
7. Do 8 trot-to-canter transitions (every 20 strides) each direction.
8. Repeat Step 4.
9. Finish with a walk for 2 to 5 minutes on straight lines (this may mean leaving the round pen).

TIP: This session flows best when you're able to make smooth and efficient transitions between tasks. For this reason, it is recommended to have your horse on a longe line as opposed to moving at liberty in the pen.

WORKOUT 5
Round Pen Rally

4.7 A-D Walking in straight lines outside the round pen (A), Lateral Yields (B), Tight Serpentines (C), and Back-Up (D).

DURATION: Approximately 30 minutes

KEY EXERCISES USED: Lateral Yields (p. 31), Tight Serpentines (p. 34), and Back-Up (p. 27)

BENEFITS: This routine will be most successful when you're able to accomplish clear changes of trotting speeds plus correct durations of canter. Use your time during Step 1 in ways that wake the horse up and get him tuned in to you.

HOW-TO:

1. For 10 minutes: Walk the horse somewhere outside the round pen. During this time, incorporate Lateral Yields, Tight Serpentines, and walk-to-stop transitions as you wish. Proceed to round pen.
2. For 5 minutes: Slow jog around perimeter of pen. Change directions every 3 circles.
3. For 2 minutes (each direction): Energetic or fast trotting around perimeter.
4. Back up 10 steps; pause. Repeat sequence 3 times.
5. Do 10 trot-to-canter transitions (every 20 strides) in each direction.
6. For 1 minute (each direction): Sustained canter around perimeter.
7. Repeat Step 4.

TIP: Feel free to modify task durations slightly if the horse begins to anticipate direction changes, since there are several of them in this routine. If he offers unrequested changes, put him back on task and add 30 seconds to your current exercise.

WORKOUT 6
Round Pen Circles

DURATION: Approximately 35 minutes
BENEFITS: Frequent direction changes and variations in circle sizes makes this routine a highly effective use of time and small spaces. The conditioning effects of these alterations far outweigh those of an unchanging circle.

HOW-TO:

1. For 10 minutes: Brisk walk around the perimeter of the round pen. Change direction every 3 circles.
2. For 5 minutes: Brisk trot around the perimeter. Change directions half-way through. Stay active and energetic.
3. For 2 minutes (each direction): Perform small circles of 8 to 10 meters at a slow jog.

4.8 A & B Frequent changes of direction (A) and circle size (B) transform everyday circles in a round pen into a bona fide workout.

4. For 1 minute (each direction): Canter around the perimeter of the round pen.
5. Repeat Step 3.
6. Repeat Step 4.
7. For 2 minutes (each direction): Small circles at a walk.
8. Finish with 2 minutes of brisk trotting around the perimeter of the round pen.

TIP: Due to the duration of this workout, and continuous circling, a large (60-foot) round pen is best. Be sure to use a rope that allows you to quickly and smoothly shrink and enlarge your circle size. If the rope is too long, or too fat in your hands, you are likely to become disorganized with all the adjustments needed in this routine.

WORKOUT 7
Terrific Trotting Poles (Groundwork Variation)

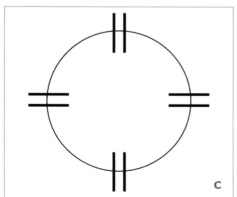

4.9 A–D Tight Serpentines (A), Turn-on-the-Forehand (B), Clockface Poles (C), and Turn-on-the-Haunches (D).

DURATION: Approximately 35 minutes

KEY EXERCISES USED: Tight Serpentines (p. 34), Turn-on-the-Forehand (p. 32), Clockface Poles (p. 37), and Turn-on-the-Haunches (p. 33)

BENEFITS: The focus of this workout is concentrated and propulsive execution of trotting ground poles, with a warm-up and rest activities to support it. Aim for a trot that is rhythmic and energetic without being rushed. Keep this consistent throughout both directions of the ground pole exercise. Be sure to set up Clockface Poles ahead of time.

HOW-TO:
1. For 10 minutes: Brisk walking, including several reps of Tight Serpentines.
2. Do 3 Turn-on-the-Forehands in each direction.
3. Do 10 reps of Clockface Poles circle in each direction at the trot.
4. Do 3 Turn-on-the-Haunches in each direction.
5. For 2 minutes: Brisk walking, in mostly straight lines.
6. Repeat Steps 2 and 3, but only 5 reps of Clockface Poles each direction this time.
7. Finish with 2 to 5 minutes of walking straight lines.

TIP: If the horse consistently knocks raised poles over, there is still value in practicing this task with poles flat on the ground. It will be more productive than the workout would be with frequent interruptions to reset poles.

WORKOUT 8

Terrain Training

DURATION: Approximately 30 minutes

KEY EXERCISES USED: Back-Up (p. 27)

BENEFITS: As with any strength workout, making efforts measurable and purposeful ensures the horse makes actual fitness gains. This especially applies to the use of hills and terrain. A mild sloping area—not steep—is ideal for this session; most pastures have a swale or something similar that can serve.

HOW-TO:

1. Back up 30 steps.
2. For 2 minutes: Walk-to-stop transitions (every 15 steps) on flat ground. Then go to the slope.
3. For 5 minutes: Wander all around the slope as space allows; walk sideways across, up and down, and diagonally.
4. For 4 minutes in each direction: Jog a large circle on the slope face.
5. For 3 minutes in each direction: Walk-to-jog-to-stop transitions repeated on the large circle.
6. To finish, walk on flat ground for 5 minutes.

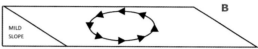

4.10 A & B Back-Up (A) and how to use a mild slope in terrain training (B).

TIP: Even in suboptimal footing, this workout can be performed with good results. If your sloping area has gopher holes, lumpy ground, or a rocky surface, feel free to modify by substituting a brisk walk for the jogging portions.

WORKOUT 9

Wide Pole Serpentines

DURATION: Approximately 30 minutes
KEY EXERCISES USED: Wide Poles (p. 47) and Back-Up (p. 27)
BENEFITS: This is a great routine to interject novelty into an established ground pole practice. To begin, be sure to set up the Wide Poles pattern (see p. 37).

4.11 A Wide Poles.

HOW-TO:

1. Do 12 reps of the following sequence: Walk over the poles, then make a serpentine that passes through the gaps between poles. Finish serpentine at the starting point to walk over the poles again.

2. For 5 minutes: Walk-trot-walk transitions (transition every 20 strides) around arena perimeter.

3. Back up 10 steps, pause 3 seconds. Repeat two more times.

4. Repeat Step 1, but only do 6 reps.

5. Repeat Step 2.

4.11 B Back-Up.

TIP: Concentrate on helping your horse bend his head, neck, and body in the direction of each curve of your serpentines in Steps 1 and 4. It is also beneficial to spend time leading the horse from both the left and right sides (still traveling in the same direction) during this workout. You can change sides halfway through Step 1 and 4, or alternate sides with each rep.

WORKOUT 10
2-Mile Hike

DURATION: Approximately 40 minutes
KEY EXERCISES USED: Turn-on-the-Forehand (p. 32), Back-Up (p. 27), Turn-on-the-Haunches (p. 33), and Lateral Yields (p. 31)
BENEFITS: When a horse walks energetically and purposefully, it should take about 18 minutes to cover a mile. During times when circumstances prevent riding, the 2-Mile Hike in-hand is a useful stand-in for a trail ride. It is short enough to be done during poor weather but long enough to offer productive stimulus for the horse.

HOW-TO:

1. For 5 minutes: Do 6 reps each of Turn-on-the-Forehand, Back-Up 6 steps, Turn-on-the-Haunches, and Lateral Yields 10 steps in each direction.

2. Walk down a road or trail at a *brisk pace.*

3 Keep walking uninterrupted for 2 miles, or for approximately 35 minutes.

4.12 A–E Turn-on-the-Forehand (A), Back-Up (B), Turn-on-the-Haunches (C), Lateral Yields (D), heading out on a 2-mile walk (E).

TIP: If it is a new—and slightly worrisome—experience for your horse to cover trail miles in-hand, try to stick with it. After a few practices, your horse will learn the ropes. Take comfort in knowing this is not a dramatic outing. You are simply walking away from the barn for 18 minutes and then back toward it. This is excellent to practice, regardless of conditioning benefits!

WORKOUT 11
Groundwork Intervals

DURATION: Approximately 35 minutes
BENEFITS: Most useful when reintroducing a horse to aerobic exercise following long layoffs, this workout is modified by lengthening or shortening the *rest phase* of each interval, based on your veterinarian or equine physical therapist's guidance.

4.13 Diamante trots on a large longe circle.

HOW-TO:

1. For 10 minutes: Brisk hand-walk, mostly straight lines. Then move to an area suitable for longeing.
2. For 1 minute: Trot on a large circle.
3. For 1 minute: Walk on a large circle.
4. Repeat Steps 2 and 3 for 5 times in each direction.
5. Finish by hand-walking for 5 minutes on mostly straight lines.

TIP: Circles in this workout should be a minimum of 20 meters, and ideally larger.

WORKOUT 12
Canter Intervals

4.14 A–D Turn-on-the-Haunches (A), Turn-on-the-Forehand (B), Back-Up (C), and do not rely on feel—use a timing device for canter intervals (D).

DURATION: Approximately 30 minutes

KEY EXERCISES USED: Turn-on-the-Forehand (p. 32), Turn-on-the-Haunches (p. 33), and Back-Up (p. 27)

BENEFITS: When building locomotive power through groundwork, the physiologic benefits of canter can often be more successfully achieved through short intervals of quality work versus "chasing" the horse around in a sustained canter with diminishing returns.

HOW-TO:

1. For 10 minutes: Brisk walking, including 6 reps each of Turn-on-the-Forehand, Turn-on-the-Haunches, and Back-Up (6 to 8 steps). Then move to an area suitable for longeing.
2. For 1 minute: Canter on large circle.
3. For 30 seconds: Walk on a large circle.
4. Repeat Steps 2 and 3 for 5 times in each direction.
5. Finish by hand-walking for 5 minutes on mostly straight lines.

TIP: Circles in this workout should be a minimum of 20 meters, and ideally larger. Be sure to keep an eye on the clock during the 30-second walk intervals. These periods are meant to be no longer than half the duration of each canter bout.

WORKOUT 13
Hillside Freestyle (Groundwork Variation)

4.15 A Sophia practices changing stride lengths on a mild slope.

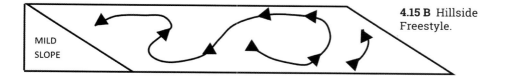

4.15 B Hillside Freestyle.

MILD
SLOPE

DURATION: Approximately 35 minutes

BENEFITS: This groundwork version of a ridden exercise from chapter 6 (see p. 108) is useful for young horses or those in advanced stages of movement rehabilitation. It offers tremendous benefit for developing body control. Through numerous small bouts of stimulus, it recruits both stabilizing *and* locomotive muscles.

HOW-TO:

1. For 15 minutes: Warm up with walking and easy trotting on flat ground, either in-hand or on a longe line. Then proceed to a mild slope.
2. For 15 minutes, perform a repeating circuit of the following tasks:
   - Serpentine up and down the slope.
   - Walk sideways across the slope face.
   - Lengthen and shorten the horse's strides while walking up and down the slope.
   - Make small *and* large circles on the slope face.
3. Finish with 5 minutes of brisk walking on flat ground.

TIP: For this workout, choose the gaits—or combination of them—that suits your horse's current ability. The exercise works at walk, jog, slow canter, or a smattering of all.

WORKOUT 14
Hill Hikes

DURATION: Approximately 35 minutes

KEY EXERCISES USED: Lateral Yields
(p. 31)

BENEFITS: This workout comes with a
disclaimer of improving both horse *and*
human fitness! Be sure to have your
walking shoes on. Use whatever sloped
surface is most accessible, though
a moderate slope creates the best
results. This is a simple but productive

4.16 A & B Lateral Yields (A) and remember, hills are not just for riding! They can be part
of groundwork, too (B).

session that can usually be performed on a driveway, in a pasture, or on a neighbor-hood hillside.

HOW-TO:

1. For 10-minutes: Hand-walk on flat ground; include a few Lateral Yields in each direction. Then head to the hill you plan to use in your workout.
2. For 1 minute: Walk briskly up the slope; turn around and walk slowly back to the bottom.
3. Repeat Step 2 for 10 reps.
4. For 30 seconds: Perform walk-to-stop transitions on your way up the slope; turn around and walk briskly back to the bottom.
5. Repeat Step 4 for 6 reps.
6. Finish by walking 5 minutes on flat ground.

TIP: Be sure to keep the horse's head and neck aligned very straight in front of his body. It is common as handlers struggle uphill themselves to tighten the lead rope in a way that curves the horse's head toward them. Avoid doing this as it twists the horse's body during activities where we are trying to strengthen him.

5

Strength Routines (Short But Serious)

Due to the concentration of workload, *strength-based workouts* are relatively short. When stimulus is applied in consolidated efforts, the necessary load to create adaptations is usually accomplished by 10 to 20 minutes of cumulative work.

Unlike with human athletes, gains are often unrealized by taking horses to the point of total fatigue during strength sessions. Instead, accumulated stress of connective tissues can lead to dysfunction. Rather than making positive gains, the horse accumulates wear and tear. Ligaments are especially susceptible to strain and overload once muscles reach fatigue. The goal is to tax the horse *nearly* to the point of fatigue but not push past the line of diminishing returns.

For this reason, the duration of each exercise and the outline of the workout should be followed closely. Unless you are working with a coach to modify workouts to meet specific requirements, do not extend the length of reps. This can be tempting if you and your horse enjoy a particular routine or you want to spend several minutes refining a certain aspect of the overall performance. Remember, workout days are not for nit-picking or schooling new skills.

Did You Warm Up?

Prior to each workout in this chapter and the next, you will need to warm up. Remember, this means *at least* 10 minutes of brisk walking, followed by 5 to 10 minutes of livelier gaits. You might choose to modify one of the Groundwork routines we covered in chapter 4 (p. 40), ride in the arena, or hack around the fields and roads. Just be sure to prime the horse's body before starting the clock on a workout.

"Hard" Workout Days: Why and When

Once a fitness foundation is in place, *hard efforts* do wonders for a horse's body. In this case, "hard" does not mean that the effort is mentally stressful or painful, or that you are teaching the horse a complex new skill. It means you are helping the horse's body reach its full athletic capacity in small repeatable bouts that lie outside the normal efforts of everyday schooling and training. Beyond improving the strength of muscles, it improves their function. Hard efforts require more from the metabolic system and leave it better able to "fire" and fuel all muscle fiber types; they improve muscles' ability to fully activate, to generate power, and to shuttle away acidic waste byproducts of forceful contractions. Routine experiences like the ones I explain in this chapter make the body not only stronger but more efficient, metabolically and physically.

Aside from these mechanical benefits, hard efforts improve the connections between muscles and the nerves that control them. They sharpen communication between muscles and their sensory and motor nerves. You can think of this as ensuring all the "electrical wiring" is hooked up and working well. This is especially crucial in cases where horses have done a lot of repetitive schooling. When a horse is ridden in an arena daily, for example, at the same energy levels, performing similar tasks, neuromuscular connections weaken. In our electricity analogy, the wires become corroded or loose. They need to be retightened and cleaned so the lights come on brightly as opposed to flickering.

Another value of hard intensity efforts is their brevity. Because they occur within a relatively short duration, they produce conditioning results while minimizing repetitive stress on the horse's body.

The productivity of hard workouts becomes negligible unless they are performed on a regular basis. This consistency is what allows adaptations to stack up on each other week by week and lead to measurable physiological gains. Aim to do a hard workout every 6 to 10 days. Many riders find it helps to have the same designated day weekly, while others allow it to float around within 10-day windows.

Respiration Considerations: Does Your Horse Huff and Puff?

At some point, most riders aboard a horse that is breathing heavily will draw a conclusion about the horse's fitness. Respiration, though, can be a fickle fitness marker. Respiratory rates are *always* telling us something important. The key is figuring out *what* the message is. It might sometimes tell you more about a horse's mental state, physical tension, or plain old natural aptitude than his current fitness.

An unfit horse will indeed breathe heavy and hard when exercised. Our goal with better conditioning is to see the horse perform the same degree of exercise with very little elevation in his respiratory rate. Occasionally, however, a well-conditioned horse will still get winded when exercising at only a moderate level. This is explained by several factors, including the need to shed heat, a humid environment, underlying fatigue, a stressed immune system, dehydration, carrying extra weight, or poor air quality.

Most often when a horse with reasonable fitness begins "panting" during a routine trail outing or arena session, he is hot and trying to cool down. This is especially true for senior horses and naturally heavy-bodied breeds. It would be a miscalculation to automatically assume in this case that the horse is not fit enough for the task at hand and activity should be ceased.

Instead, the horse's heart rate is a more accurate indicator of fitness, and it can be a good idea to take a reading and compare it with his breathing rate. If the heart rate is in a normal range but the horse is breathing hard, he is likely just hot. Does this mean you should stop what you are doing? Not necessarily. Make a habit of recording the time it takes your horse to regain a normal resting respiration rate when you pause activity. A horse's average respiration rate at rest is between 8 and 20 breaths per minute. In hard efforts, it can briefly jump to 100. When he is hot, a horse will take rapid shallow breaths to dissipate heat. A time for concern is if breathing becomes labored, irregular, or it *remains* higher than his heart rate.

If he regains a resting rate within five minutes, it is generally fine to carry on with your ride. If on the other hand he keeps breathing heavily for well over 10 minutes (and his heart rate is in a normal range), it is worth stopping and figuring out ways to modify your schedule to exercise him without generating so much heat. Can he lose some weight? Can you ride when it is cooler outside? Can you pre-cool the horse by wetting his body before riding?

If his heart rate is not in a normal range *and* he is "panting," he has exceeded his fitness level.

Common Alternative Causes of "Shallow Breathing"

When a horse does not breathe rhythmically and deeply or does not blow out through his nose regularly throughout a ride, or makes little grunting noises at trot and canter, his respiration becomes compromised. This means less oxygen is taken in and shuttled—along with blood—to working muscles, which in turn leads to faltered nerve signals. Put simply, the horse cannot move with ease and balance, and the programming for correct movement will not take place.

Checking Your Horse's Pulse (Heart Rate) and Respiration

You can do a quick check of your horse's pulse (heart rate) and respiration with your own hands.

To take a pulse reading, place your fingers under the horse's cheek near the back of the jawbone. Feel for a large artery. When you push on this artery, you will feel the pulse throbbing. Count the number of pulses that happen in 15 seconds. Multiply this number by "4" to determine the horse's current heart rate in beats per minute (bpm).

To determine respiration, stand near his flank and observe his ribcage expanding with each breath. Each inhale and exhale counts as a single breath. Count the number of breaths in a 15-second period, and then multiply times "4" to determine current respiration rate.

Any number of factors might cause a horse to hold his breath during exercise, including tension and anxiety. Common explanations include conformational issues, sore feet, and muscular imbalances. Regarding conformation, horses with wide jowls or thick poll muscling can suffer when asked to work in a collected frame. The *nasopharynx* and *larynx* can become obstructed due to this extra fleshiness and impair airflow. Similarly, blockages in the lower cervical vertebrae can compromise the *phrenic nerve*, which exits in this area. This is a major nerve that controls breathing. The nervous system's communication to the diaphragm then weakens, along with oxygen uptake and utilization.

The diaphragm has attachment points along the lower back and rear portion of the ribcage. If a horse has overly tight *loin muscles* or *intercostals* between his ribs, the action of the diaphragm will be hindered. Sometimes horses that were worked too early in collection also have tension or imbalance in the *scalene muscle* at the base of their necks. This muscle helps stabilize the ribcage *and* plays a role in respiration. If it cannot function well, the horse will move with short choppy strides and shallow breaths.

These are just a few of the most commonly restricted areas among shallow breathers, and I offer them as a starting point for your own exploration of whether your horse is breathing in a way that leads to better mechanics and fitness.

Tips for Gauging Your Horse's Respiration

Take note of how long it takes your horse to first blow through his nose during any session. Is it within the first 5 minutes? Excellent! Is it longer than 25 minutes? Uh-oh, he is holding his breath.

Listen to your horse's breathing when cantering. Mother Nature wired a horse's nervous system to breathe during canter by coupling his breathing rate with his stride rate in a 1:1 ratio. For every canter stride, the horse needs to breathe in and out once. The exhale should be audible. Imagine the forceful, rhythmic exhalations of a galloping racehorse.

One of my mentors is fond of saying that when your horse blows through his nose, it is like he gives you a bouquet of flowers. I enjoy counting how many bouquets of flowers I can accumulate during a ride. This metaphor captures the beauty and pleasure of a horse that is moving well by breathing well.

Success Story

I have known Bentley, a sweet and wonderful Missouri Foxtrotter, for several years. He has spent some time at my barn for training and attended occasional clinics. During the COVID-19 pandemic, I lost touch with him and his owner. As it turned out, his owner developed health issues that prevented her from riding Bentley and eventually led to her realization that she needed to find him a new home. In the meantime, as the pandemic carried on, Bentley spent a full year out of exercise. Except for occasional jaunts to a larger paddock for turnout, he spent his days just hanging out.

When his owner brought Bentley to my barn to recondition in preparation for sale, I started with a one-month buildup of walking and groundwork. I progressively increased the duration of our walks and added complexity to our groundwork routines. At the end of that month, we started ridden work, mostly at a walk. Gradually, we added measured amounts of trotting.

Toward the end of the second month, The 1:1 strength workout (p. 79) became a staple. It provided a way to increase fitness without the risk of overexertion due to the brevity of intervals. When done weekly, it also allowed me to assess how Bentley felt and whether it seemed like he was becoming more efficient at the routine. Initially, I modified The 1:1 to be done at a strong trot, and then later, we moved on to a canter.

I am very happy to report that Bentley regained a good level of fitness and then found a wonderful new home.

Succeed, Move On

Your horse's needs plus your own preferences will undoubtedly guide which strength workouts you choose. A general rule is to tackle each workout for two weeks in a row before moving on to a new one. This allows you to reap the most out of the routine through sufficient practice but without letting output become rote. Feel free to revisit favorite workouts every two months or more, but don't make a habit of repeating them more often than that.

And remember, the goal is to deliver various dosages of stimulus for the purpose of gaining strength and fitness. It is not to perform tests in a perfect manner. There *will* be times that the horse's coordination and balance get lost, there *will* be ground poles that get knocked over or stepped on, there *will* be moments when the horse might become hesitant and need encouragement. There might be even more less-than-pretty scenarios that arise. They are not reasons to quit or to decide your horse doesn't like a certain task. They are reasons to pet the horse on the neck, smile, and enjoy the athlete taking shape underneath you.

WORKOUT 15

The 1:1

5.1 Heather and Sabra gallop for one-minute bursts.

DURATION: Approximately 46 minutes

BENEFITS: These high intensity intervals belong in every rider's toolbox. They are worth revisiting any time you are building fitness. If they are new for you, begin with just 8 reps; if you're already seasoned at the prescribed 10 reps I note in the instructions, do 12 reps. This routine is best performed in a very large arena or field, or on a track.

HOW-TO:

1. For 15 minutes: Warm up with plenty of lively trotting and transitions between walk, trot, and canter.

2. For 1 minute: Gallop.
3. For 1 minute: Rest at trot.
4. Repeat Steps 2 and 3 a total of 10 times, no stopping or walking.
5. Finish with 3 minutes of slow jogging followed by 8 minutes of walk.

TIP: If you and your horse are unfamiliar with galloping, perform these intervals at the fastest canter you can muster.

WORKOUT 16

Wide Pole Serpentines (Ridden Variation)

DURATION: Approximately 35 minutes
KEY EXERCISES USED: Wide Poles (p. 37), Lateral Yields (p. 31)
BENEFITS: By adding speed, we target muscles with more propulsion than the groundwork version of

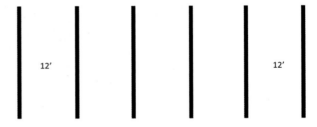

5.2 Wide Pole Serpentines.

Wide Poles. Set up the Wide Poles pattern ahead of time. When performed uninterrupted, these workouts put muscles under load without full rest for a relatively brief but focused time.

HOW-TO:

1. For 12 to 15 minutes: Warm up, primarily limbering up and walking/jogging.
2. Do 12 reps of the following sequence: Trot across the poles, then make a serpentine that passes through the gaps between poles. Finish the serpentine at the starting point to cross poles again.

3. For 2 minutes: Speed changes at trot (slow to very fast, and repeat) around the perimeter of an arena or a field.
4. Repeat Steps 2 and 3.
5. Finish by walking for 5 minutes, including several Lateral Yields in each direction.

WORKOUT 17

The 4x3

5.3 Diamante and I speed through a 3-minute canter interval before a short walk break.

DURATION: Approximately 45 minutes

BENEFITS: Hard aerobic efforts are followed by ample recovery periods in this workout, which is best done in an open field or very large arena. The goal is to really move out while making minimal turns/corners. These gallop sets strengthen propulsive muscles.

HOW-TO:

1. For 12 to 15 minutes: Warm up at walk and easy trot.
2. For 3 minutes: Fast canter.
3. For 2 minutes: Rest at walk.
4. Repeat Steps 2 and 3 a total of four times.
5. Finish with 5 minutes easy trotting plus 5 minutes walking.

TIP: If your own stamina is challenged by this workout, try riding in two-point. Be mindful that you do not slow the horse down to make the ride easier if you get winded.

Terrific Trot Poles

DURATION: Approximately 55 minutes

KEY EXERCISES USED: Clockface Poles (p. 37)

BENEFITIS: The variety of gaits plus repeated bouts of ground poles requires good effort from the horse's gymnastic muscles, while simultaneously loosening him up. Set up the Clockface Poles exercise ahead of time.

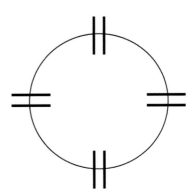

5.4 Clockface Poles.

HOW-TO:

1. For 12 minutes: Warm up, riding mostly straight lines with numerous changes of speed within all gaits.
2. Do 12 reps of Clockface Poles in each direction.

3. For 1 minute (each direction): Brisk canter around the arena perimeter.
4. Do 8 reps of Clockface Poles in each direction.
5. Repeat Step 1.
6. Finish with 8 minutes of easy jogging and walking.

TIP: Each clean execution of the pattern counts as a single rep. Reps where the horse knocks over poles or wanders off the geometry are not counted.

WORKOUT 19
Canter Clock

DURATION: Approximately 35 minutes
KEY EXERCISES USED: Clockface Poles (p. 37)
BENEFITS: This is a canter variation of Terrific Trot Poles (see p. 82). To begin, set up the Clockface Poles pattern with the following modification: place a single pole (not two) at each quarter mark of the circle.

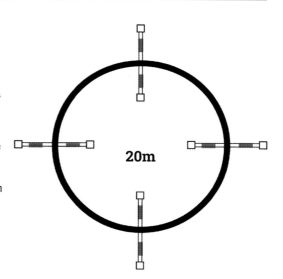

20m

5.5 Canter Clock.

HOW-TO:
1. For 10 minutes: Warm up walking.
2. For 5 minutes: Warm up trotting.
3. For 2 minutes (each direction): Canter speed changes (slow to very brisk, and repeat continuously), around the perimeter of the arena.
4. Do 10 reps of cantering Clockface Poles on your right lead.
5. For 1 minute: Rest at walk.
6. Do 10 reps of cantering Clockface Poles, left lead.
7. For 1 minute: Rest at walk.
8. Finish with 5 minutes of easy jogging and 10 minutes of walking.

TIP: If your horse consistently knocks over the raised poles, ride the workout with poles on the ground versus having to stop frequently to reset the raised setup. These workouts are most effective when they can be performed seamlessly, one task flowing to the next, so choose the pole setting that allows this while still challenging your horse.

WORKOUT 20
Agile Athlete

DURATION: Approximately 30 minutes

KEY EXERCISES USED: Agile Athlete (p. 38)

BENEFITS: This workout combines numerous effective components— transitions, cavalletti, and energetic gaits. The great Olympian Ingrid Klimke has demonstrated the centerpiece of this workout in numerous clinics as benefiting horses across all disciplines. Here, we combine the exercise with active rest periods on straight lines to challenge the horse to recover without full cessation of activity. Set up the Agile Athlete pattern on a 30-meter circle ahead of time.

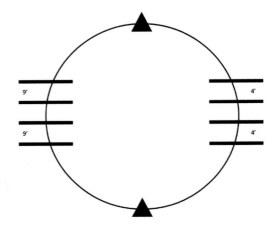

5.6 Agile Athlete.

HOW-TO:
1. For 12 minutes: Warm up.
2. For 3 minutes: Canter speed changes (slow to very fast every 20 strides) around the perimeter of the arena.
3. Do 10 reps of the Agile Athlete pattern on the left lead.
4. For 2 minutes: Trot perimeter of arena.
5. Do 10 reps of the Agile Athlete pattern on the right lead.
6. For 2 minutes: Canter speed changes around the perimeter of the arena.

7. Finish by trotting easy for 5 minutes and then walking on a loose rein for 10 minutes.

TIP: If you struggle to achieve consecutive clean reps (that is, the workout is interrupted by the knocking down and resetting of the raised poles), add 10 reps of just trotting poles at the end of the session to ensure effectiveness of the activity.

WORKOUT 21
Speed Play

5.7 A Heather and Sabra finish an interval of slower cantering...

5.7 B ...and then they hit the accelerator for 1 minute.

DURATION: Approximately 40 minutes

KEY EXERCISES USED: Raised Uneven Poles (p. 36)

BENEFITS: Bursts of propulsive power are paired with the eccentric muscle work to tune up overall function—control and recruitment, fuel pathways, and resilience. This is a simple and straightforward workout suitable for any decent-sized arena. If needed, this workout can be modified for trotting, so long as the energy and work efforts are high.

HOW-TO:

1. For 12 minutes: Warm up, including 20 repetitions of walking over Raised Uneven Poles, plus some easy trotting.

Set 1:

2. For 2 minutes: Slow canter on the left lead.
3. For 1 minute: Very brisk canter on the left lead.
4. For 90 seconds: Rest at walk.
5. Repeat Steps 2 and 3 on the right lead.
6. For 2 to 3 minutes: Walk break before beginning Set 2.

Set 2:

7. For 1 minute: Very brisk canter on the left lead.
8. For 1 minute: Slow canter on the left lead.
9. For 1 minute: Very brisk canter on the left lead.
10. For 2 minutes: Rest at walk.
11. Repeat Steps 7 through 9 on the right lead.
12. Finish with 5 minutes of easy jogging and 5 minutes of walking on a loose rein.

TIP: A good execution of this workout depends on very distinct speeds and efforts of the gait. For "slow canter," for example, aim to canter as slowly as your horse is able, as though a person could walk beside you on the ground without you passing by.

6

Hills and Terrain Routines
(More Mileage That's Mild,
Less Steep and Deep)

Hills offer indisputable conditioning potential, but their benefits rely on approaching them with a plan that is relevant to a goal. In the case of building strength, there is no guarantee of results by making your horse occasionally climb inclines that leave him winded and sweaty. When using terrain to strengthen locomotive muscles, slope angles and repeatability of efforts, plus strategic rest intervals, play an enormous role.

By itself, traipsing around steep terrain with a hope of strengthening the horse often brings cardiorespiratory improvement without intended strength. This is due to hills being too steep and encouraging poor form or overexertion, insufficient repetitions, unproductive work-to-rest ratios, or working past fatigue. Due to the sheer physical challenge, climbing steep hills often contributes to asymmetrical movement patterns and pushes the horse to an anaerobic metabolic rate that does not support the muscle fiber recruitment and adaptations sought for bettering locomotion and balance. Further, eccentric muscle loading, which happens during descents, produces more metabolic waste (acidic buildup, "burning" sensation) than other types of fitness activities, and can lead to poor function and recovery.

Take heart if you lack access to steep hills. Aside from very specific conditioning goals, steep climbs are generally not used for strength workouts targeting basic strength gains. Also, rest assured that you do not need access to miles of hilly terrain. In fact, many of the following workouts prefer mild slopes that allow for repeatable dosages. An ideal slope angle will require the horse to change his center of gravity, flex his joints more, and engage his topline and bottom-line muscle chains with greater force. Most pastures have a swale or rise that fits this description.

For the purposes of clarity and prescription, the workouts in this chapter use the following profiles.

10 Mild Slope—A gentle uprising that progressively gains height; terrain gains 6 to 8 vertical feet over 100-foot distance. Many driveways and pastures fit the description.

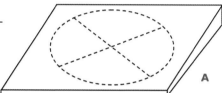

11 Moderate Slope—This requires more effort; the horse needs to use shorter, more powerful strides to ascend. Heart and respiratory rate will increase notably after a few hundred feet. Terrain gains 8 to 10 vertical feet over 100-foot distance.

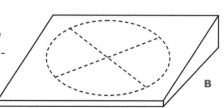

12 Steep Slope—A type of hill that requires automobiles to downshift to lower gears; terrain gains 15 to 20 vertical feet over 100-foot distance.

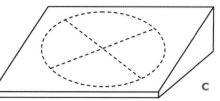

6.1 A–C Mild slope (A), moderate slope (B), and steep slope (C).

If you lack access to slopes that fit these exact profiles, perhaps you have at least a gentle upswell, berm, or ditch. The longer uphill reps cannot be performed in this case, but the workouts that call for maneuvering around and across a mild slope certainly can.

Modifications

In-Hand

Several of the workouts in the pages ahead could be adapted to perform in-hand if that works better for your terrain and your horse's current level of training or fitness. When modifying for this purpose, be sure to keep the horse's neck aligned straight in front of his body rather than curved toward you. The horse's body needs to be aligned when training on slopes or there is the possibility of strengthening asymmetrical movement, rather than achieving the fitness goals you want.

Rehab Cases

Many of these hill workouts can also be modified to serve horses in physical rehab. By adjusting reps and overall duration, they offer good settings for reawakening neuromotor activity, proprioception, and body control. Work with a vet or sports therapist to modify the routines to fit within a prescribed rehab plan.

Senior Horses

Owners of senior horses often wonder if or when they should stop riding hills. My advice is to really listen to your own individual horse. First, no unfit senior should be ridden up and down hills. Without fitness, the effort of hills brings a lot of strain and the possibility for negative forces on joints. Especially in the case of arthritis, a horse should have at least a little fitness before enjoying hilly rides. When fitness exists, hills are not *necessarily* an uncomfortable experience for an older or arthritic horse. My general rule is to let each horse tell you. Most horses will get to a point where they can no longer ride hills, but this might be a lot later than you expect. Do not pre-emptively decide your horse is too old to ride on hills until he or she has given you very clear reasons. If you treat horses like they are "old" by limiting activities based on their numeric age, they will become old. If, on the other hand, you read their bodies and attitudes

Success Story

HoneyB was a four-year-old Mustang with stifles that locked and slipped so much that her owner was beginning to worry she had no future. HoneyB's owner liked to ride on remote backcountry trails in Utah and Montana, and she had hoped HoneyB would develop to be her next trail mount. But whenever the little mare trotted or stepped laterally, her stifles locked, and she did not want to move. She became reluctant to be ridden, and the quality of her movement did not improve, even though her owner tried to address the issue. She had been advised to "ride hills," but without clearer prescriptions to follow, HoneyB got worse instead of better.

Her owner reached out to see if I had any ideas. I suggested she take a more progressive approach to HoneyB's conditioning. While hill work was indeed the goal, I wanted to ease into those efforts after laying a foundation of exercises that would require stability from HoneyB's stifles but not irritate them. I recommended a plan that included two weeks of daily groundwork emphasizing exercises like Step-Ups (p. 28), Raised Uneven Poles (p. 36), and an increasing number of Back-Up steps, plus 2-Mile

Hikes in-hand (p. 64). Following this, HoneyB's plan shifted to incorporate pre-ride mobility drills and light riding daily. Most of the riding at this point was done at walk with controlled segments of easy jogging. By Week Four, we also began incorporating mild hill workouts at the walk. Specifically, I recommended The 45/20 (p. 97) and Zigzag Hills (p. 96). By the end of Week Four, HoneyB's trail outings, which were on mostly flat terrain, were up to nearly 3 miles, and she was fulfilling all activities without stifle problems. Now we had a foundation we could build on.

For the next four weeks, we adjusted HoneyB's plan to increase the duration of each session, add more trotting and some cantering, and incorporate a weekly workout from this chapter. HoneyB continued to absorb the training with positive results and offer good energy. I am happy to report that at the time of writing, she and her owner were planning a summer of long trail rides in Montana, and her stifles were giving her no problems.

and fitness levels, as opposed to their years, they might not "act their age" until past a surprising point.

The signs I look for to determine if hills should be avoided with an older horse are *consistent* expressions of discomfort or struggle. This includes a persistent unwillingness to travel down hills straight (that is, the horse always wants to shift his hindquarters to one side), an inability to maintain steady rhythm down hills, excessive tripping and stumbling, an abnormally high heart rate on moderate slopes, and repeated balkiness. When these kinds of signs show up repeatedly, it might be a good time to avoid hills and to make fitness gains with other routines. Or it might be time to seek out different gradients. Even if your horse can no longer ride steep slopes, it does not mean that mild ones are out of the question.

Rider's Role

A general rule of thumb when riding slopes is to keep your own body parallel with nearby trees. This will mean a *slight* incline or recline of the torso, depending on the angle of your slope. This is not an exaggerated lean; it will hinder the horse to move your weight far ahead or behind his center of gravity near the withers.

Also pay attention to the position of your lower leg. It is common, when riding with long stirrups, for the lower leg to swing forward near the horse's shoulders when descending hills. This is disadvantageous to the horse as it causes the rider's seat to sink more heavily into the back of the saddle. Adding pressure or tension here impedes the ability of the horse's hind legs to step freely forward under the horse's body. Similarly, when riding up hills, riders who lean too far forward inadvertently swing their lower legs back toward the horse's flanks. As a result, these riders tip more weight toward the front of the saddle, sometimes clenching with their knees, and end up ahead of the horse's center of gravity. Our goal when riding hills should be to remain as balanced in the saddle as possible without an exaggerated lean either forward or backward. We also want to keep our heels below our hips rather than displacing our legs forward or backward. Hills are hard enough for horses; we do not want to add burden by requiring the horse to find balance under our own misaligned bodies.

Horse Form

As with most training exercises, the horse will benefit most from being in good balance and posture on hills. This does not mean he should look like an advanced dressage competitor, but we also do not want him lollygagging around with a hollow topline or his neck twisted to one side or hanging down to the ground. An ideal posture allows the horse to bear weight equally over all four legs and to shift weight easily from front end to hind end, *and* vice versa. For most horses, this is a posture where the topline is horizontal to the ground, with poll and withers and sacrum nearly level. This is sometimes referred to as a *natural balance*, or one that resembles an elongated, gently arched rainbow.

Adapt to Your Terrain

Many of the following workouts ask you to travel up and down the same slope. Depending on your situation, this might not be possible. Your hill might be too narrow to turn around on or perhaps your footing might get slippery with repetitive travel. Or maybe your horse gets antsy and unsettled by repeating the same terrain up and down. It might suit you better to plan these workouts somewhere that allows you access to a sequence of hills nearby rather than trekking up and down the same one. If this is the best option, do it even if it means your interval durations might not match the workout assignment. It is far better to modify the workout slightly to fit your situation than to skip it. The same applies to the steepness of your terrain. If a workout asks for a moderate slope but you only have a mild one, just go ahead and use what you have. There is still value in the structure, timelines, and tasks given in each workout even if your available terrain does not entirely match the description. So go ahead, get creative, and get out there.

WORKOUT 22
Slope Figure Eights

6.2: Slope Figure Eights (A). During rests between work sets, halt your horse facing down the slope (B).

MILD
SLOPE

DURATION: Approximately 40 minutes

SLOPE: Mild

BENEFITS: Ride the figure-eight pattern on the side of a hill with as much precision as you would in the arena, aligning the horse's spine to the inward curve of each arc on your figure. This requires the horse to frequently adjust his balance and stabilize his trunk and pelvis. It is dependent on the horse paying close attention to his rider's seat cues.

HOW-TO:

1. For 12 minutes: Warm up on flat ground (arena, road, or field). Then proceed to the slope.
2. For 3 minutes: Jog a figure-eight pattern across the face of the slope.
3. For 10 seconds: Rest at a halt, facing your horse downhill.
4. Repeat Steps 2 and 3 twice more.
5. Finish by walking 8 minutes on flat ground (arena, road, or field).

TIP: If the footing quality is suboptimal or your horse seems initially wary and unbalanced, modify by walking sections of the figure. For instance, jog the uphill portions and walk the downhill portions, or keep transitioning between strides of both gaits until you're able to sustain a steady jogging rhythm. With some skilled footwork, this workout can also be performed as groundwork.

WORKOUT 23

Slope Circles

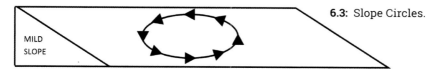

6.3: Slope Circles.

MILD
SLOPE

DURATION: Approximately 40 minutes
KEY EXERCISES USED: Back-Up (p. 27)
SLOPE: Mild
BENEFITS: By requiring the horse to make frequent postural adjustments, this ridden version of the Terrain Training Workout from chapter 4 activates stabilizing muscles while strengthening larger gymnastic muscles.

HOW-TO:

1. For 10 minutes: Warm up on flat ground, including several reps of backing up and transitions between walk-stop-trot. Then proceed to a hill with a mild slope.

2. For 5 minutes: Walk briskly in all directions on the slope: sideways, diagonally, up and down.
3. For 4 minutes (each direction): Jog a large circle on the slope face.
4. For 10 seconds: Rest at the halt, facing the horse uphill.
5. Repeat Step 3.
6. Finish with 5 minutes walk on flat ground.

TIP: Depending on your available terrain, aim to ride an approximately 20-meter circle in Steps 3 and 5; modify by enlarging if needed.

WORKOUT 24
Zigzag Hills

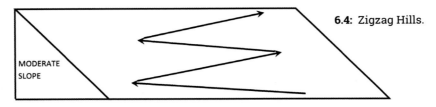

6.4: Zigzag Hills.

MODERATE
SLOPE

DURATION: Approximately 30 minutes
KEY EXERCISES USED: Lateral Yields (p. 31)
SLOPE: Moderate
BENEFITS: By shifting the horse's line of travel, we interrupt any tendency to overuse the front end, and hindquarter engagement improves.

HOW-TO:
1. For 10 minutes: Warm up on flat ground with plenty of Lateral Yields to establish bending and responsiveness from the horse. Also include a few minutes of jogging. Proceed to the moderate slope.
2. For 1 minute: Walk briskly uphill, performing a tight zigzag pattern; turn around, and walk straight back downhill to your starting point.

3. Repeat Step 2 a total of 10 times.

4. To finish, jog for 5 minutes on flat ground, then walk 5 minutes.

TIP: After the initial few reps, be sure to remain precise with your geometry. Every zig and zag should be sharp and discernible. Be sure you are not just wandering from side to side. Do not allow your horse's form to get sloppy or his walk to become sluggish.

WORKOUT 25

The 45/20

6.5 A: I ask Diamante for ground-covering strides heading uphill.

6.5 B: Coming down the slope, I ask for shorter steps and a more collected posture.

DURATION: Approximately 36 minutes

SLOPE: Moderate

BENEFITS: While faster gaits would be favored for cardiovascular improvement, a purposeful walk effort can lead to fuller muscle recruitment by avoiding assistance from inertia.

HOW-TO:

1. For 15 minutes: Warm up on flat ground, including 5 minutes of speed changes (slow, medium, fast) at trot. Then head to your slope.
2. For 45 seconds: Very lively, extended walk strides uphill. Then turn around.
3. For 20 seconds: Walk downhill with shortened, collected strides.
4. Repeat Steps 2 and 3 a total of 12 times with no pauses.
5. Finish with 8 minutes of trotting and cantering on flat ground.

TIP: Going uphill, encourage the horse to extend his neck out and downward, with his poll below his withers. Going downhill, encourage the horse to walk with a rounded topline, with his poll at—or higher than—his withers. Envision energetic staccato steps. Note that this session can also be modified for groundwork.

WORKOUT 26
Simple Straights

6.6 Heather maintains a rhythmic jog up the slope.

DURATION: Approximately 40 minutes

SLOPE: Moderate

BENEFITS: When bracketed by a suitable warm-up and cooldown, 1-minute uphill intervals are a fitness staple for performance horses. If your slope is steeper than a moderate incline, modify to perform this workout at a brisk walk. Otherwise, do it as prescribed.

HOW-TO:

1. For 12 minutes: Warm up on flat ground, then proceed to the slope.
2. For 1 minute: Jog straight up the slope; turn around.
3. For 1 minute: Walk briskly down the slope.

4. Repeat Steps 2 and 3 a total of 10 times without pausing.
5. Finish with 8 minutes of walking and jogging on flat ground.

TIP: Focus on creating a jog that is rhythmic and steady going up the slope versus one that surges between speeds. Follow the time allotment when walking downhill—you will not necessarily return to your starting point.

Transitions on a Slope

6.7 Backing up a slope requires balance and strength in the horse.

DURATION: Approximately 50 minutes

KEY EXERCISES USED: Back-Up (p. 27)

SLOPE: Moderate

BENEFITS: The format of this workout allows for creativity; you are asking the horse to make various transitions while traveling up and down the slope. The exact number and frequency of transitions depends on the length of slope and quality of footing you have access to.

HOW-TO:

1. For 15 minutes: Warm up on flat ground and include a few minutes in each walk, trot, and canter. Then proceed to the slope.
2. For 2 minutes: Proceed up the slope, riding frequent transitions between walk and jog. Turn around.
3. For 1 minute: Proceed down the slope, riding frequent transitions between walk, stop, and backing up (four steps).
4. Repeat Steps 2 and 3 a total of 8 times.
5. Finish with 5 minutes of brisk trotting on flat ground, followed by 5 minutes of walking.

TIP: Crookedness is a common tendency after initial reps of backing up while descending the slope. The horse will often shift his hips askew from the line of travel, rendering the exercise less valuable. Do your best to keep the horse's body aligned, and if needed, modify by taking fewer backward steps.

WORKOUT 28
Power Hills

6.8 After a 1-minute canter up the slope, Diamante will get a long walk recovery before the next interval.

DURATION: Approximately 61 minutes

SLOPE: Steep

BENEFITS: These are high-intensity efforts; be sure the horse has already performed a few of the preceding workouts without undue stress or depletion. This workout targets propulsive power in the hindquarters. Push the horse hard on the uphill; he will get a nice long recovery after each rep.

HOW-TO:

1. For 15 minutes: Warm up on flat ground, including plenty of energetic trot bursts and cantering. Then proceed to your slope.

2. For 1 minute: Canter briskly up the slope; turn around.

3. For 5 minutes: Walk down the slope.

4. Repeat Steps 2 and 3 a total of 6 times.

5. Finish with 10 minutes easy walking and jogging on flat ground.

TIP: If you reach the bottom of your hill before the 5-minute mark, continue walking on flat ground until the full rest period is up. For fit and well-seasoned horses, the number of reps can be increased to 8 or 10.

WORKOUT 29
Sustained Hills

6.9 A Amy and Joe jog up a long slope.

6.9 B Walking down the slope serves as active recovery from the work effort.

DURATION: Approximately 56 minutes

SLOPE: Mild or moderate

BENEFITS: Longer intervals at moderate work intensities provide the stimulus for muscular endurance, which improves fatigue resistance and aptitude for collected movements. In these longer interval reps, the downhill walk recovery period is twice the duration of each uphill work effort. To perform this routine, you will need access to quite a long slope.

HOW-TO:

1. For 10 minutes: Warm up on flat ground at a brisk walk followed by 5 minutes of trotting. Then proceed to the hill.
2. For 3 minutes: Jog up the slope; turn around.

3. For 6 minutes: Walk down the slope.

4. Repeat Steps 2 and 3 a total of 4 times.

5. Finish by walking for 5 minutes on flat ground.

Collection + Extension

6.10 I ask Diamante for a powerful energetic walk up the slope before turning around to jog back down.

DURATION: Approximately 35 minutes

SLOPE: Mild

BENEFITS: This simple workout uses terrain to flex the horse's hind joints and strengthen the muscles that support them. This result comes from the downhill jog intervals. Note that these intervals make this workout unsuitable for young or green horses that are still developing basic balance.

HOW-TO:

1. For 15 minutes: Warm up on flat ground with plenty of transitions between all gaits. Then proceed to the slope.
2. For 1 minute: Extended walk uphill; turn around.
3. For 30 seconds: Jog straight down the slope.
4. Repeat Steps 2 and 3 a total of 8 times.
5. Finish with 3 minutes trotting plus 5 minutes walking on flat ground.

TIP: Maintain a very slow jog pace. If the horse rushes, weight and concussion will increase on the forefeet, which should be avoided.

WORKOUT 31

The Hilly Ride

DURATION: Approximately 60 to 90 minutes

SLOPE: Mixed

BENEFITS: Depending on the duration of a trail ride, conditioning effects from hills can be diminished by:

- Overall fatigue from total distance of the outing.
- Excess recovery time between each hill effort.

Uneven terrain requires the horse to adapt his center of gravity, shifting it either forward or back. This creates tone and harmony in the muscle chains along the top and bottom line of the horse, which is critical for functional athletes. To use a hilly ride as a strengthening tool, follow the guidelines in the instructions below.

HOW-TO:

1. For 15 minutes: Warm up on flat terrain before hitting the first hill.

6.11 Amy and Heather head out on a hilly ride.

2. For 45 to 75 minutes: Go out on the hills, following this general rule: *If the hills are steep, ride shorter; if they are mild, ride longer.*

3. Choose a route that allows you to spend a third of your total time ascending or descending slopes. Depending on the terrain, this might include one or two very long hills or numerous small rolling hills.

4. Mix things up in terms of gaits—keep the horse's efforts below his heart rate threshold, though (see p. 74).

5. Perform low-intensity gaits between each slope.

TIP: Remember not to gauge the success of hilly rides by the horse's cardiorespiratory effort. Depending on many factors—slope angle, humidity, bodyfat, and more—a horse may or may not become winded and sweaty. This does not determine strength gains. (See p. 88 for more on this subject.)

WORKOUT 32
Hillside Freestyle

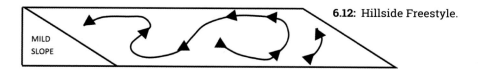

6.12: Hillside Freestyle.

DURATION: Approximately 35 minutes

SLOPE: Mild to moderate

BENEFITS: There is not a "right" or "wrong" way to execute the following exercise circuit, meaning you can arrange exercises in any order. The point is to give the horse a constant need to adapt and organize his body to the changing balance and slope angle. You will be traversing up, down, across, and around the slope to continuously change the horse's effort.

HOW-TO:

1. For 15 minutes: Warm up with walk and easy trot on flat ground, either riding or longeing. Then proceed to the slope.

2. For 15 minutes: Perform a repeating circuit of the following tasks without pauses:

   • Serpentine up and down the slope.
   • Walk sideways across the slope face.
   • Lengthen and shorten strides while walking up and down the slope.
   • Perform small *and* large circles on the slope face.
   • Transition between gaits.

3. Finish with 5 minutes of brisk walking on flat ground.

TIP: For this workout, choose the gaits—or combination of them—that suits your horse's current ability. The exercise works for walk, jog, a bit of slow canter, or a smattering of all.

WORKOUT 33
Power Surges

6.13 Diamante and I burst up the hill before our walk recovery, heading down.

DURATION: Approximately 40 minutes

SLOPE: Moderate to Steep

BENEFITS: Combining speed and resistance, short uphill surges can recruit *fast-twitch muscle fibers*. This benefits activities that require moments of explosive strength, such as high-level collection, accelerations, sprints, and riding fast obstacles. It also contributes to metabolic efficiency, allowing the athlete to shift between different muscle functions and energy pathways.

HOW-TO:

1. For 15 minutes: Do an energetic warm-up.
2. For 10 seconds: Gallop uphill, going "all-out."
3. For 45 seconds: Walk downhill at a calm, easy pace.
4. Repeat Steps 2 and 3 a total of 10 times.
5. For 3 minutes: Rest at walk or easy jog, ideally on flat ground.
6. Repeat Steps 2 and 3 for 3 more times.
7. Finish with easy riding on flat ground for 10 minutes.

TIP: Due to the repetitive format, some horses might begin getting squirmy through anticipation on the downhill walk rests. Be sure to keep them straight and aligned through their bodies, even if that means getting their minds to settle and slow down by adding a few halt transitions. Alignment is key during strength sessions!

CHAPTER 7

Sample Fitness Schedules (What's Right, When)

The "De-Trained" Horse

As discussed at the beginning of this book, horses begin to lose measurable amounts of fitness after a decline in exercise lasting approximately four weeks. In this case, "decline in exercise" is defined as *training fewer than three days per week*. This also applies to horses living in pasture, though their loss might be slower over the coming weeks, depending on their movement patterns while in the field. Existing fitness continues to erode up to 12 weeks, at which point horses are entirely "de-trained." In some locations, inclement weather imposes these de-training periods. For others, injury or illness interrupts their training routines.

A horse that has de-trained *must* be reconditioned progressively. The following schedule can be followed in these cases.

BASIC FITNESS SCHEDULE5

WEEK 1	• 5 days x 30 minutes brisk walking in-hand
WEEK 2	• 1 day x brisk walking in-hand 30 minutes • 3 days brisk walking under saddle 30 minutes
WEEK 3–4	• 1–2 days x fitness-based groundwork (p. 41) • 3 days x riding 30–40 minutes, $\frac{2}{3}$ time walking, $\frac{1}{3}$ time trotting
WEEK 5	• 4 days x riding 30–40 minutes, $\frac{1}{2}$ time walking, $\frac{1}{2}$ trotting, very brief canter • 1 day x fitness-based groundwork routine
WEEK 6–7	• 4 days riding 40 minutes in all gaits • 1 day x ridden workout (pp. 72 and 88)
WEEK 8–12	• 3 days riding/schooling 40 minutes • 1 day x ridden workout • 1 day x long low-intensity session, 70–90 minutes

TIP: After 12 weeks, programs can be tailored to be sport-specific. This includes adjustments to daily intensity levels, adding double sessions on given days, and adding workouts to the weekly schedule. In cases where horses have been laid up for longer than four weeks but less than 10, the schedule can be started at Week 3.

Gait Dysfunction and Anomalies

When a horse struggles with a chronic weakness of some kind that affects his quality of movement, the best plan is to briefly give up the horse's current and habitual routines to access the underlying issue. This means removing the horse from his current daily activities or schooling and following the schedule I offer here. In this schedule, "therapy exercises" are defined as *postural and corrective exercises prescribed for your specific horse by a vet, therapist, or trainer*. For optimal effectiveness, new exercises should be substituted every two weeks. (Note: Some of the exercises in this book can be used as therapy exercises, as can those in my book *55 Corrective Exercises for Horses*.)

This plan can be especially helpful in scenarios where a horse is not lame but is also "not quite right" in his movement. Perhaps the horse moves with a peculiarity or restriction but you cannot find a diagnosis, or maybe he has been in some kind of pain that got treated but left behind a certain oddity of locomotion.

GAIT DYSFUNCTION AND ANOMALIES FITNESS SCHEDULE
Protocol for addressing instability and improving movement patterns

WEEK 1–2	• Therapy Exercises + 20 minutes continuous low aerobic activity x 4–6 days, *twice daily*
WEEK 3–4	• Therapy Exercises + 30 minutes continuous low aerobic activity x 4–6 days
WEEK 4–6	• Therapy Exercises + 40 minutes of moderate aerobic activity, ideally including all gaits x 4–6 days

TIP: In this context, *low aerobic activity* is low-stress, easy exercise: simple patterns and plenty of straight lines. *No skill schooling. Therapy exercises* can play a more gymnastic role (examples include ground poles, gradients, and surface and terrain changes). They should remain specific to your horse's particular need.

Trail Riding

Have you ever wondered what it might take to get your horse really fit for trail riding adventures, or how to go about progressively conditioning him to do something like an endurance ride or multi-day trail excursion? This conditioning schedule solves the guesswork. It will bring your horse to a level of cardio and musculoskeletal fitness to comfortably and enjoyably complete a 25- to 30-mile trail event, whether you want to do a competitive trail ride, an endurance race, or an ambitious riding and camping adventure. Or maybe you just want to follow a fitness schedule to improve your horse's handiness and athleticism on the trails. This schedule guides you day by day through building fitness in a way that is achievable and sustainable.

Some basic guidelines:

- This program is built on cumulative volume of consistency of aerobic activity. Aside from the weekly interval workouts, the daily rides are not intended to be high intensity. Most of your trail rides can be done at an average speed of 6 miles per hour, except where noted in the schedule. For most horses, this is a slow trot. Trail rides of 6 miles or less on the schedule can be replaced with a 45-minute arena session when you prefer.

- You are welcome to add up to 2 days per week of extra light work (such as longeing) over what is prescribed in the schedule, but be sure to include 2 rest days per week. It is best when these days are not consecutive.

- If you cannot follow the prescribed days of exercise exactly each week, try to follow the distribution of work similarly—that is, do not do your interval workout and your long ride on consecutive days.

- Most weeks in this program include an interval workout. These are best performed somewhere with consistent and good footing like your arena. The intervals follow a 1:1 ratio of work to active rest, meaning you spend 1 minute working *hard* (cantering or trotting fast) immediately followed by 1 minute of jogging slowly (do not walk; it is

7.1 Trail fitness comes from cumulative gains of consistent workload, plus strategic sessions of higher intensity.

important here to train the horse's cardiovascular system to recover). Use a watch; do not rely on your own estimations of time. Each work-rest bout counts as one rep. For example, if your training schedule says to do 1:1 intervals x 8, this means you will canter for 1 minute and then jog for one minute (1 rep) and you need to do 8 of these reps, so repeat the sequence 7 more times to fulfill your workout.

• These workouts should be preceded by a 15-minute warm-up and 15-minute cooldown of your own design.

15-WEEK TRAIL-RIDING FITNESS SCHEDULE
Progressive conditioning for trail riding and endurance

WEEK ONE						
Monday	Tuesday	Wednesday	Thursday	Friday	Saturday	Sunday
	4 Miles		4 Miles		6 Miles	

WEEK TWO						
Monday	Tuesday	Wednesday	Thursday	Friday	Saturday	Sunday
4 Miles		4 Miles			6 Miles	

WEEK THREE						
Monday	Tuesday	Wednesday	Thursday	Friday	Saturday	Sunday
	4 Miles		6 Miles		8 Miles Hilly Ride	

WEEK FOUR						
Monday	Tuesday	Wednesday	Thursday	Friday	Saturday	Sunday
	6 Miles		6 Miles		8 Miles Hilly Ride	

WEEK FIVE						
Monday	Tuesday	Wednesday	Thursday	Friday	Saturday	Sunday
6 Miles	1:1 Intervals x 6		8 Miles		10 Miles Flat & Quick 1.5 Hours	

WEEK SIX

Monday	Tuesday	Wednesday	Thursday	Friday	Saturday	Sunday
6 Miles	1:1 Intervals x 6		8 Miles		10 Miles Slow & Steady	

WEEK SEVEN

Monday	Tuesday	Wednesday	Thursday	Friday	Saturday	Sunday
	6 Miles Hilly Ride	4 Miles			12 Miles Hilly Ride	

WEEK EIGHT

Monday	Tuesday	Wednesday	Thursday	Friday	Saturday	Sunday
5 Miles	1:1 Intervals x 6		6 Miles		8 Miles Slow & Steady	

WEEK NINE

Monday	Tuesday	Wednesday	Thursday	Friday	Saturday	Sunday
5 Miles	1:1 Intervals x 8		8 Miles		12 Miles Flat & Quick	

WEEK TEN

Monday	Tuesday	Wednesday	Thursday	Friday	Saturday	Sunday
7 Miles	1:1 Intervals x 10		5 Miles Hilly Ride		10 Miles Hilly Ride	

WEEK ELEVEN

Monday	Tuesday	Wednesday	Thursday	Friday	Saturday	Sunday
6 Miles	1:1 Intervals x 12		6 Miles Hilly Ride		12 Miles Slow & Steady	

WEEK TWELVE

Monday	Tuesday	Wednesday	Thursday	Friday	Saturday	Sunday
	5 Miles	7 Miles	6 Miles Hilly Ride		16–18 Miles Intersperse 3-Minute Intervals of Quick Throughout	

WEEK THIRTEEN

Monday	Tuesday	Wednesday	Thursday	Friday	Saturday	Sunday
4 Miles		6 Miles			12 Miles Slow & Steady	

WEEK FOURTEEN

Monday	Tuesday	Wednesday	Thursday	Friday	Saturday	Sunday
	6 Miles	4 Miles	1:1 Intervals x 6		8 Miles Brisk Pace	

WEEK FIFTEEN

Monday	Tuesday	Wednesday	Thursday	Friday	Saturday	Sunday
	4 Miles Slow	30 Minutes Easy Exercise (such as Longeing)	6 Miles Hilly Ride	2 Miles Slow	EVENT Target Goal, Event, or Deadline	

PART FOUR:
FINAL THOUGHTS

8

Conditioning
Considerations
(Takeaways and Tips)

Surfaces Play a Role in Fitness

Without access to multiple riding surfaces, many horses plateau in their fitness or get stuck in a state of physical discomfort. In fact, different footings can play such a big role in any horse's conditioning that there is an industry adage for it: *There are no poor surfaces; there is only poor use of surfaces.*

From a fitness and conditioning standpoint, there are benefits to riding on both soft *and* firm surfaces. If you are limited to training on only one type of footing weekly, chances are good that your horse's musculoskeletal system has some deficiencies. For both injury prevention *and* gymnastic conditioning, training purposefully on surfaces allows you to modulate physical effort while attuning proprioception. This leads to physical resilience while optimizing muscular and skeletal strength.

Put very simply, soft sandy terrain requires more muscular and aerobic effort while firm ground develops better proprioception, limb coordination, and hoof stimulus. While an ideal scenario includes training on both firm and soft footings throughout each week, horses that are grappling with gait dysfunction or mild lameness may benefit from fully changing their primary training area for a period.

Firm Footing

Any new surface types should be introduced slowly in 10- to 15-minute periods for an initial three weeks, and this principle applies to harder ground like packed dirt, clay, decomposed granite, asphalt, and other concussive footings. During these small intro sessions, the horse's body adapts by sustaining microscopic damage to subchondral bone and then remodeling. Fatigue fractures and lesions occur when the remodeling process cannot keep up with the rate of damage, in instances when horses were not progressively adapted. In most cases, this adaptation process is a worthwhile undertaking that offers big value to your horse.

Horses training predominantly on soft footings like arenas develop loss of proprioception over time. This leads to compromised sensory feedback to the nervous system and eroded neuromuscular patterns. Being stabled on soft shavings or straw further contributes to this *sensory dullness*.

Even if they avoid injury, a number of these horses experience sub-optimal muscular function: altered firing patterns, delayed contractions, fewer fibers recruited. Their physical conditioning often seems to hit a wall or backslide. Changing the training environment can help avoid these plateaus.

In rehab settings, stimulus from firm ground serves a key role in optimizing the horse's neuromuscular system to return to training. Likewise, hard surfaces contribute enormously to young horses' bone and hoof health as well as ligament and tendon resilience.

For students with limited access to a variety of surfaces beyond the arena, positive stimulus from firm ground can come in the form of hand-walking for 20 minutes three times per week on the driveway or barn aisle or a quiet paved road. A weekly trail ride typically offers horses a chance to tread on packed roads or sun-baked paths as well.

An exception to the value of firm ground applies to horses with navicular pain. Hard surfaces do not allow the toe of the hoof to sink in when pushing off, creating pressure in the navicular region. For horses without existing conditions, this can lead to resilient adaptations in the hoof. But for those dealing with problems, it can exacerbate soreness.

Soft Footing

Soft or deeper footing is typically defined as measuring 3 or more inches. Regardless of material—sand, synthetic fibers, shavings, and so on—soft footing allows the hoof to partially sink down before pushing off. Work of this kind requires more physical effort. Put simply, muscles work harder to lift and move limbs. Dry sand is especially taxing in this respect as the looseness underfoot requires even more exertion. Horses working on this kind of footing have recorded heart rates up to 50 percent higher when compared to firmer surfaces.

From a basic aerobic conditioning standpoint, therefore, soft surfaces offer a good tool. Also, when needing to build up gymnastic muscles, this kind of footing helps. For example, during rehab and conditioning plans for stifle stability, controlled work on soft ground is often prescribed following an initial period of stationary calisthenics. The effort of propelling the horse through deeper footing delivers its own resistance training.

This is also frequently beneficial to help young horses with "scrambling" canters find more balance. The effort of treading through slightly deeper footing helps engage, rather than brace, their back and hindquarters while their strides benefit from slower break-overs. The helps reduce rushing tendencies.

For students with access to only a packed area (less than 1-inch depth) to ride, it is worth finding or creating a soft area to longe or ride on at least two days per week. This could be a round pen or a path filled with shavings out in the field or a sandy paddock.

Very few riders have access to state-of-the-art footing. But the good news is that it matters more to have a *variety* of footings, and to use them mindfully.

Conditioning Young Horses

Should young horses be left in pasture to "grow up" or brought in to begin their training? While arguments can be made in favor of each plan, the ideal approach is actually somewhere in the middle. In order to enjoy athletic lives later on, youngsters *do* need regular exercise, but the structure of that training should differ from a mature horse's. Primarily, it should be shorter, slower, and avoid concussive skeletal forces.

Physiological studies have shown that horses receiving appropriate exercise in the first three years of life are better adaptedand commonly sounder—during their riding and driving careers later when compared to horses that were not exercised until their third or fourth year. Yes, young, entirely pasture-raised horses are primed well for general health. But from a future athletic perspective, these youngsters benefit from *additional structured exercise* that is appropriate and progressive for their stage of development. As soft tissues like tendons and ligaments grow in these initial years of life, they are highly responsive to exercise stimulus. This means that while they are forming and growing, they can add power and elasticity and resilience based on input received from exercise. In other words, exercise leads to the development of higher quality tissues. For most breeds, this opportunity of responsiveness diminishes significantly after the third year.

Rather than being deleterious, early exercise has a protective effect on the horse's musculoskeletal system over the long term. It develops stronger *musculoskeletal structures*—ligaments, tendons, muscles. This in turn allows bones and joints to mature without undue stress. Further, early exercise helps muscles make adaptations to aerobic stimulus, leading to more efficiency down the road. During this phase, muscles become adept at *metabolizing energy*—storing oxygen and using fat as a fuel source. Their capillary networks enlarge and mitochondria density improves. This sets up the mature horse to meet the demands of discipline-specific training without strain or poor muscle function.

From a mental *and* physical perspective, leaving a horse basically untouched until his third year is more harmful than maintaining a small steady diet of exercise all along. Most vets nowadays agree that gentle exercise can be introduced to yearlings and continued until they are started under saddle. But a young horse's regime does have special considerations. This means owners and trainers need to think outside the box in terms of what a daily training session might look like. It should not just be an abbreviated version of what older horses in the stable are doing. In addition to the number one rule that *all youngsters should spend the majority of their time living outside in a pasture and moving around naturally*, the basic principles for young-horse exercise are as follows:

- Implement brief but frequent sessions (10- or 15-minute sessions daily, or a couple of these "mini sessions" per day, three times per week).
- Focus on general movement, nothing sport-specific.
- Allow plenty of time to pause and process what they're doing (and rest tissues) during any session.
- Avoid skeletal concussion (this includes hard ground, repetitive circles or longeing, jumps, and sharp turns or lateral exercises).
- Avoid exercises involving excessive speed or intensity.
- Do not restrict the neck in any particular frame. Allow the horse to find a neutral balance on his own, which ensures that the vertebrae at the base of his neck, which are still growing and forming in the early years, will not be compromised.

Taking all this into account, what might these "mini training sessions" look like? The activities on the following pages meet the positive criteria for one- to three-year-old horses. These can each be a session on their own or mixed and matched to add novelty. With some creativity, you will no doubt come up with your own as well.

Ground Poles

While you want to avoid the concussive forces of jumping or going over raised poles, you *do* want to introduce your youngster to tasks that require him to organize his body and adjust his foot placement. This builds neural pathways that will lead to higher athletic capability later on. With poles arranged in various positions on the ground, practice sequences of walking across and around and between them. I like to spend a focused 10-minute walk-only session doing this a couple of times per week. As the horse grows and develops, some days he will seem much more coordinated than others, and that is perfectly okay. If he initially seems apprehensive or trips over poles, make creative patterns wandering between and around them at first.

Controlled Wandering

Rather than longe youngsters around repetitive circles, which torques their lower limbs and developing joints, I recommend what I call "controlled wandering" on a longe line. This involves traveling around an arena or field combining a variety of loopy circles and straight lines. By walking quickly or jogging alongside the horse, you're asking him to sync up with your strides and mirror your movements around a large area. This way, you're getting the exercise benefit that comes with longeing but without the negative physical consequences.

Ponying and Trail Hikes

The simple activity of continuous walking at a prescribed pace offers numerous benefits for a young horse. Leading him in-hand on power hikes or ponying him alongside another horse helps him develop a rhythmic gait, creates proprioceptive gains on changing terrain, and makes good use of straight lines (as opposed to detrimental repetitive circling) for exercise. As a general rule, aim to travel at least a mile or for 20 minutes. So long as your youngster is not too anxious, however, you can walk up to 4 miles on these outings. Whether you are leading or ponying, be sure to change sides periodically in order to mitigate asymmetry in the horse's body posture.

Another option, besides a mile or longer outing, is to get your youngster out two or three times per day for a brisk walk up and down the driveway for 10 minutes continuously. These consistent doses of exercise result in positive adaptations over the long haul. It is also a useful way to introduce the practice of shortening and lengthening his steps as you ask.

A young horse's early training exercises should be simple, short, and consistent. Consistency of positive bone and soft tissue stimulus is what leads to a sounder, saner athlete down the road. Remember, the goal is plain and straightforward *movement*, not sport-specific training or lathered sweaty workouts. Let yourself be creative, and enjoy the fact that you are setting the horse up for a less stressful performance life.

Index

Page numbers in *italics* indicate illustrations.

K

Klimke, Ingrid, 84

L

Lameness, 113, 121. *See also* Gait
  dysfunction
Lateral Yield exercise, 31–32, *31*
Leg, of rider, 92
Ligaments, 72, 123
Longeing, 41, 44, 125
Lyme disease case study, 51

M

Metabolic function, 9, 73
Mitochondria density, 9, 123
Mobility Magic workout, 53–54, *54*
Mobility routines, 17, *18*, 19, 53–54
Movement
  benefits of, 125
  quality of, 113
  volume, *16*
Muscles and muscle function, 8–9, 23, 73,
  88–89, 121

N

Navicular pain, 122
Neck
  balance role, 9
  restriction/bending of, 71, 90, 124
Needs of horse, assessing, 11–12, 17
Neuromuscular coordination, 8–9

O

Obstacles, in active rest, 17
The 1:1 workout, 79–80, *79*

P

Pastured horses, 8–9, 111, 123, 124
Pauses, during workouts, 15, 43, 47–48
Pelvis, stability of, 9
Performance efficiency, 3, 73–74
Plateaus, in conditioning, 121
Poll, *18*, 76
Ponying, 125
Postural muscles, 23
Power Hills workout, 102–103, *102*
Power Surges workout, 109–110, *109*
Pre-Ride Circle exercise, 35, *35*
Proprioception
  exercises for, *11*, 23, 121
  as fitness type, 10
  in pastured horses, 8
Prusik knots, 44, *45*

Q

Quality, vs. quantity, of work, 67, 74

R

Raised Uneven Poles exercise, 36, *36*
Range of motion, 19
Reconditioning, 77, 112
Recovery, 49–50
Rehabilitation, 21, 48, 90, 121
Release, by horse, *28*
Repetitive activity, in performance
  efficiency, 3, 13
Respiration
  as fitness marker, 74, 107
  monitoring, 75
  shallow, 75

U

Up and Over exercise, 30, *30*

V

Value/vigor, of exercise/workouts, 11–12

W

Walking
  benefits of, *16*
  hand-walking, 17, 47, 50, 122
  as warm-up, *22*
Wandering, controlled, 125
Warm-up, 21–24, *22*, 48, 73
Weakness, chronic, 49–50
Weather, inclement, 46–48
Weekly planning, 13–14
Wide Pole Serpentines workout
  groundwork variation, 63–64, *64*
  ridden variation, 80–81, *80*
Wide Poles exercise, 37–38, *37*
Workouts
  daily doses, 48

double sessions, 20–21
duration and intensity of, 14, 15, 50, 74, 78
fitness schedules, 111–118
Groundwork routines, 52–71
"hard," 73–74
Hill and Terrain routines, 94–110
horse's posture in, 93
injury/weakness considerations, 49
preparation for, 2, 5–6, 47–48
selection of, 48–49
Strength routines, 79–87
vs. training, 3, 73–74
value and vigor of, 11–12
weekly planning, 13–14, 78

Y

Young horses, 121, 122, 123–125

Z

Zigzag Hills workout, 96–97, *96*